MIND RENEWAL

BIBLICAL SECRETS TO A BETTER YOU

LEOSTONE MORRISON

Extra MILE Innovators
Kingston, Jamaica WI

.   .   .   .   .

Published by
Extra MILE Innovators
54 Montgomery Avenue,
Kingston 10, Jamaica W.I.
www.extramileja.com
ruthtaylor@extramileja.com
Tele: (1876) 782-9893

Print and eBook by
N.D. Author Services [NDAS]
www.NDAuthorServices.com

Cover Design by
Cardo Design
cardodesigns02@gmail.com

AUTHOR CONTACT
restorativeauthor@gmail.com

Scripture verses unless otherwise noted are quoted from the authorized King James Version of the Bible.

DEDICATION

To my mother, Albertha Mitchell. Despite immense poverty, you stayed the course. You raised three boys and two girls as a single mother. You didn't have much but you gave us everything.

To my wife Sherene Badjnaut Morrison, my strength, my confidant and friend. Your sincere love gives me the extra confidence to pursue who God ordained me to be.

To my four sons, Shamari, Caleb, Josiah, and Khadeem, and my daughter Gabriella, you are my inspiration from God.

ENDORSEMENTS

In the last century a popular American clergyman, Norman Vincent Peale, published an influential book entitled *The Power of Positive Thinking."* It changed the lives of very many. One conservative scholar, who was not satisfied with the biblical content, quipped "Frankly, I find Paul appealing, and Peale appalling!"

The author of this book, *Mind Renewal,* writes in the genre of Peale's bestseller, and, as the subtitle suggests, he tries his best to strike that happy balance between divine revelation and popular application. It reminds me much of gems like Isaiah 26:3 and Philippians 4:8; it is still true that "as man thinketh..., so is he". After all, I'm not what I think I am. What I think, I am. Hope you will find this tome appalling—sorry!—appealing.

—Dr. Delano Palmer
Former Deputy President
Jamaica Theological Seminary

. . . .

In *Mind Renewal,* Pastor Leostone Morrison helpfully reminds us that our words, inasmuch as they align with God's Word, have the power to shape our vision, thoughts, and attitudes.

In turn, our vision, thoughts, and attitudes influence both how we live in the present and the future. He provides salient personal illustrations and practical examples. I am thankful Pastor Morrison wrote this book and am confident it will challenge, encourage, and in-spire many to grow in their Christian faith.

—Rev. Dr. Paul A. Hoffman
Senior Pastor of EFC Newport

. . . . .

Mind Renewal offers the key to unlock mental and spiritual freedom for those who have put limits on themselves consciously and unconsciously. It elevates the mind and awaken the spirit to the possibility of real fulfilment and purpose.

—Rev. Dalton Grenyion
Senior Pastor
Sandy Point and
St. Paul's Wesleyan Holiness Church

. . . . .

Leostone Morrison has written a must-read transformational book for anyone seeking untapped hidden mysteries of the Word of God. This was such an insightful and sound revelation of the spiritual dimension of the mind...Read this brilliant piece of work—and you will see truth unravelling in front you.

—Latoya Clarke, Founder
Undiluted Love Ministries

Acknowledgements

To the Holy Spirit my primary Destiny Helper. Thank you for imparting to me the wisdom to write this Mind Renewal manual. As you downloaded to me, I have recorded to share with the world.

I am truly honored to be blessed with the family I have. Sherene my wife, you permitted me time and space to write. Your priceless support and encouragement, cannot be monetarily valued.

My friend Hillary Dunkley Campbell, you have been a significant source of motivation. You pressed me to not slump under the weight of the voice of past-procrastination. Your contribution is recorded in heaven and I sincerely believe your reward will be great. My family and all who will read this book, say thank you.

Thank you Jacob Munakwa Ngumbah for encouraging me to convert my Bible Study teachings into book format. You saw the wealth of what the Holy Spirit was teaching and thought it wise to be preserved.

Mrs. Latoya Clarke Grant, for your endorsement and behind the scene contributions which are too many to mention. I pray you will continue to make yourself available to the Kingdom of God.

Continuous appreciation for the Next Level Let's Climb Bible Study Family. Although we are countries apart, we connect in one room via WhatsApp. Thanks to the prayer warriors who have kept my family and I in prayer, interceding on our behalf perpetually. Those who accepted the challenge to critique a chapter, your contributions are priceless.

To Ms. Cameka Taylor, Authorpreneur and founder of Extra MILE Innovators and the Indie Authorpreneurs Group, for the "From Idea to Manuscript in 30 Days" Challenge. This is the vehicle the Holy Spirit used in making this dream a reality. Ms. Taylor, you shared your wealth of knowledge with me, for this the world is better.

Dr. Delano Palmer, Reverend Dalton Grenyion and Dr. Paul Hoffman, I thank you for your words of endorsement. I am tremendously grateful.

I personally thank Rev. David Grant for writing the foreword for this Mind Renewal manual. It's not just acknowledgements for the book but for your unreserved investment into my life. Your challenge to me has pushed me to expand beyond the regular. Your challenge was: "If you don't do better than I have done, then you have failed." I purpose to continue pursuing that challenge by not failing you.

FOREWORD

"And be not conformed to this world but be ye transformed by the removing of your mind," seems to be the translation that so many Christians hear. Many seem to think that when one becomes born again God has no use for their minds/intellect. Considering that our thoughts determine our habits and our habits determine our lifestyle, it behooves us to think right. Never forget that as a man thinketh, so is he.

A treasure has been unearthed in the body of Christ: Leostone Morrison, and I give thanks to be a part of the journey. I have had the privilege of mentoring and pastoring Leostone for over 15 years. The author has personally experienced what he now offers to us his readers. I invite you to take this journey of life trans-forming knowledge by "Mind Renewal."

Mind Renewal is a refreshing read. It encapsulates the deep truth of how far our thoughts are from God's thoughts. There is a sharp focus on the fact that if we are going to be "successful" at this life our minds must be renewed. I do find this book to be riveting. It cap-tures your attention from the very outset. When I began reading the manuscript I could not put it down. It caused a lot of introspection.

Leostone has captured the heart and mind of God in the pages of this book. He articulates God's desire for us to think and operate in what might be considered the "God-class." Rather than seeing a vast expanse of space, see universes. I am so looking with eager anticipation to the devotional workbook that will compliment this volume to bring practical lasting change.

—Rev. David Grant
Senior Pastor
Jamaica Evangelistic Centre
Odigia Services, Visionary and Founder

TABLE OF CONTENTS

Foreword i

Introduction: The Cost of Freedom 1

Chapter 1: Coexisting in the Present and the Future 5

Chapter 2: The Word-Seed 13

Chapter 3: Praying vs. Commanding 25

Chapter 4: The Promised Word 35

Chapter 5: Great Spirits and Mediocre Minds 43

Chapter 6: Perspective and Mind Renewal 53

Chapter 7: Cracked Performers 61

Chapter 8: Victory Beyond the Barriers 71

Chapter 9: The Success Ladder 83

Chapter 10: A Better Me 93

Chapter 11: It's Not About You 103

Chapter 12: What is Your Reality? 119

Chapter 13: Divine Purpose 129

Chapter 14: Beauty of Scars 149

Chapter 15: Your Next 163

Chapter 16: Marah to Elim 181

Chapter 17: Overcome 189

Chapter 18: Coming to Yourself 207

Afterword: Going Forward 217

Closing Prayer 221

References 223

About the Author 227

INTRODUCTION:

THE COST OF FREEDOM

Is freedom an illusion propagandized by those in authority and propelled by the wealthy, with the lie of unity and equality for all mankind? What makes us equal or free? Am I free because the chains and yolks have been removed from the visible, but have gotten stronger in the invisible? Am I free because I remain on the outside of a maximum security facility? If a replica of a forest is created and the animals are taken from their African safari and made to roam and live in this replica, does this make them free?

Are you free when the screeching sound of your mistakes keeps echoing, as your mind hinges on broken promises and expectations? Are you free when the sun tries to penetrate the window panes, heavily tinted with sorrows, opened by pain, shut by guilt and covered by shame? Are you free when your mental capacity refuses to be effective and think in futuristic terms? Are you free when you are crippled by the events of yesterday and the dimness of today? Are you free when the earthquake that followed the hurricane, is a near memory because your heart is still populated by the debris produced, and you hope and search for a resting place? Are you searching for that place of acceptance, familiarity, and peace, but still this place seems to be constantly eluding you?

Were you overzealous or unrealistic in your desire for hopeful rewards, when you pursued mental emancipation and freedom from the prison of race, religion, politics, economics, and self? Was it too much to admit, as renowned Jamaican Dancehall artiste, Buju Banton penned in his song, "I Want to Rule My Destiny," that the "rich man's way is in the city, destruction of the poor is his poverty?" Was it too much to desire freedom?

Freedom is an illusion if the state of freedom is not enjoyed by the majority of inhabitants. Freedom is considered to be a luxury to some, a gift to others and a right to others. Freedom is the ability to maximize potential and opportunities in a constructive format without constraint.

I listened and pursued renowned Reggae singer, Bob Marley's instructions, "emancipate yourself from mental slavery, none other but yourself can free your mind." But what did I find? I am a prisoner of my own mind. The war to escape your own mind will not be won by new legislation, the firing of missiles or the signing of peace treaties, but rather by the renewal of your mind. I'm my own captive and my own deliverer, and so are you.

The greatest war is the one you face in your mind. The greatest prison is the one created in your mind. This book will entrust you with the tools to free you from that war and equip you with valuable tools that will assist you in emancipating yourself from the self-inflicting pains, and barriers you have imposed on yourself.

To bask in the wealth afforded in this life, we need to be perpetually renewing our minds, as instructed by the writer of the book Romans: "And be not conformed to this world: but be ye transformed by the renewing of your mind, that ye may prove what is that good, and acceptable, and perfect, will of God" (Romans 12:2). Renewing of the mind is the rejection of one's worldly ideologies, dogmas and belief systems to the synchronization of your mind to the complete will of God.

We understand that a person will never achieve what the mind has not perceived. Therefore this book is designed to help you to achieve your purpose and your highest dreams and aspirations. It will position you to escape the clutches of the ordinary to become the best version of yourself. To escape the clutches of ordinary, we must renew our minds and grasp the riches that awaits us outside the parameters of the norm. This is a call to think and act at a higher frequency. It is a journey to freedom via the renewal of your mind. The result will be a better YOU.

CHAPTER 1:

COEXISTING IN THE PRESENT

AND THE FUTURE

"There is no passion to be found playing small—in settling for a life that is less than the one you are capable of living." —Nelson Mandela

We have heard that the sky is the limit. This, in its rawest sense speaks to the open vast abundance of possibilities. The size of the sky varies based on the availability of one's vision, or the space one is exposed to. The person who is confined to a room with only one window, will not see the sky in the same magnitude as the person who is sitting on an open football field. With this in mind, we are forced to accept that, not everyone has the same sky. Each person's sky is dependent upon their personal world-view and ideologies. The peak of a man's ideology will be the roof or ceiling of his sky. The expanse of a man's sky will never outgrow the abundance or restriction of his belief system. Let's remove the difference of physical sight, move the person in the room with a single window and cause him to join his counterpart on the football field.

This does not guarantee equality in skies. Same space, opportunities and sight, but variations in vision. Unfortunately, *vision* and *sight* have been used simultaneously to the detriment of the true meaning of the words. Sight speaks to the utilization of one of man's physical senses by way of design while vision goes beyond what is physical and natural. It takes into thought, your capability to ruminate about the future and progresses with imagination or understanding. Vision encapsulates three dimensions: past, present, and future. The experiences of the past and knowledge of the present are coordinated into future plans and chartered courses. All three are vitally important.

Nelson Mandela said, "There is no passion to be found playing small—in settling for a life that is less than the one you are capable of living." Living a life that is less than your maximum requires no effort, and is easily achieved by forsaking vision and focusing on sight. *Vision sees beyond sight.* Vision roams the streets of the terrains where sight has failed to see. Therefore, vision is superior to sight.

Jamaica's national hero, the late Marcus Garvey said, "A people without the knowledge of their past history, origin and culture is like a tree without roots." To effectively navigate into the wealth of the future, you must have intimate knowledge of where you are coming from. We have a tendency to be selective in our past memories, choosing to remember and highlight the pleasantries while throwing away the negatives. However, as we renew our minds to truly garner the wealth of the past, which will be used in our visions for tomorrow, we must appreciate and learn from both fronts—negatives and positives. These are our experiences.

To renew your mind is to reject worldly ideologies, dogmas and belief systems and synchronize your mind to the complete will of God. As we journey on this road of life, our personal worldview continues to evolve as new experiences are added. One of my lecturers at the Jamaica Theological Seminary once said to a class: "the man who goes into the river is not the same person that comes out." What he alluded to was the man's experience. He had new knowledge which was now added to his previous dictionary of experiences. We are constantly changing as we experience life in its pain and its glory. There is a repeated mistake of persons abiding in their past experiences and missing the present and future possibilities.

Thomas Jefferson said, "I like the dreams of the future better than the history of the past." While we embrace and learn from the successes and failures of the past, we must never reside in the place of memory. The dreams of the future are the visions of our tomorrow, waiting to be discovered and enjoyed. I embrace fully Jefferson's position. The past is already done and the future is equipped with endless possibilities, just waiting to be envisioned and pursued with all diligence.

The future is like blank pages prepared to be filled with paragraphs and chapters.

The desire of many to separate the past, present, and future is not completely possible because there is continuity in our living. As we renew our minds, we must be conscious of this reality: *we are coexisting in the present and the future simultaneously.* What we are living today are actually the choices of yesterday, and what we will live in our tomorrow are the choices we make today. With that understanding, each human must be both a planter and a reaper. It goes back to basic agriculture as found in the book of Ecclesiastes.

To everything there is a season and a time to every purpose under the heaven: a time to be born, a time to die; a time to plant, and a time to pluck up that which is planted; a time to kill, and a time to heal; a time to break down, and a time to build up; a time to weep, and a time to laugh; a time to mourn, and a time to dance; a time to cast away stones, and a time to gather stones together; a time to embrace, and a time to refrain from embracing; a time to get, and a time to lose; a time to keep, and a time to cast away; a time to rend, and a time to sew; a time to keep silence, and a time to speak; a time to love, and a time to hate; a time of war, and a time of peace (Ecclesiastes 3:1-8).

The season to ensure what is reaped tomorrow, is now. This takes us back to vision. Hear what the Bible says in Proverbs 29:18a; "Where there is no vision, the people perish." While we are living in the now, we must begin to envision the future and commence its creation. Some persons have fallen in love with doing a vision board. This ranges in terms of years and is laced with their goals and expected time frame for accomplishment. They then strategically decide how they will make this their reality. This is a tactical futuristic investment. Foolish is the man who waits on the tide of the wind to carry him where it pleases. Instead, we must dictate how the matter unfolds.

We have all made blunders and wasted precious years. However, if we fail to make the necessary adjustments or changes, we will be stuck in a repeated cycle. It's not enough to have sight, vision is pivotal. Let's be cognizant that the people with sight but lacking in vision, perish. The farmer understands that if he eats all the corn today, he will have nothing to plant. This sounds simple, but as we reap today our harvest planted yesterday, we must reserve a portion to be planted for tomorrow's harvest.

A great story that captures the raw truth of living tomorrow today, is the account of Joseph in the book of Genesis. The Pharaoh had a dream which Joseph interpreted to mean, there would be seven years of plenty and then seven years of lack. Joseph advised that during the years of plenty, there be storage of crops in anticipation of the years of lack. This was done, and the nation of Egypt had enough and surplus during the years of lack. The neighbouring communities who did not prepare for the seven years of famine because of lack of vision had to depend on supplies from Egypt. You don't want to become the victim of living only in the now. While you are enjoying the blessings of the now, secure the blessings of your tomorrow. Be very conscious, that you are coexisting in the present and the future.

MIND RENEWAL KEYS

In this chapter, "Coexisting in the Present and the Future," we have shared some Mind Renewal keys to help you to become a better person. Here is a summary of these keys that you can apply to your life daily or as the circumstances arise. Read and meditate on them. Pray and declare them over your life to walk in the victory God has prepared for you.

1. Not everyone has the same sky.
2. The expanse of a man's sky will never outgrow the restrictions of his belief system.
3. To renew your mind is to reject worldly ideologies, dogmas and believe systems and synchronize your mind to the complete will of God.
4. What we are living today are actually the choices of yesterday, and what we will live in our tomorrow are the choices we make today.

5. As we journey on this road of life, our personal worldview will continue to evolve as new experiences are added.

6. The season to ensure what is reaped tomorrow is now.

7. Foolish is the man who waits on the tide of the wind to carry him where it pleases. You dictate how the matter unfolds.

CHAPTER 2:

THE WORD-SEED

"The future is within the seed."

—Apostle Joshua Selman

There is an effective futuristic tool of investment that we have yet to fully grasp: *the spoken word.* Jesus showed us several examples as He lived this truth. Let's briefly examine a few.

> For he taught his disciples, and said unto them, the Son of man is delivered into the hands of men, and they shall kill him, and after that, he is killed, he shall rise the third day (Mark 9:31).

Jesus did something here that we easily miss. He uttered a prophetic declaration: "I'm going to die, but on the third day, I shall rise." Now, this is a bold and serious futuristic investment. Jesus demonstrated to us the power of orchestrating the future while we are still living in the present. His words decided the chain of events that He would experience in the near future. He dictated the order: killed then resurrected.

When I studied at the Jamaica Theological Seminary, one of my assignments was to complete a family genogram. This was painfully done. The dysfunctions highlighted from the assignment are now being used as guidelines for making solid futuristic declarations. The old patterns must not be allowed to continue into the next generation. As I meditated on this, a question illuminated my mind which caused me to commence futuristic investments in my children's lives. They shall get married before having children. Poverty shall not be their portion and the best available education shall not be a distant desire. Their lives will be lived according to the will of God. Hear what God, the Father said in Isaiah 55:11:

> So shall my word be that goeth forth out of my mouth: it shall not return unto me void, but it shall accomplish that which I please, and it shall prosper in the thing whereto I sent it (Isaiah 55:11).

Now, Jesus is God in human form, therefore the same goes for Him. His words cannot return to Him void. He said, on the third day I shall rise. Jesus made a choice to send His Word ahead of Him into time. So before He died, the Word was already created and set in motion: resurrection on the third day. Before Jesus was crucified, His declared words already put into place all that was needed for the fulfilment of His utterance.

You should therefore be ever conscious that you are not merely uttering words, but you are putting into motion in the spirit realm, the materials needed to accomplish your desired reality. This makes it imperative for you to choose wisely that which is allowed to leave your mouth. Jesus said, "it's not what goes into the mouth that defiles it, but what comes out" (Matthew 15:11). Understand that your words are so powerful, they can defile (mar, spoil) your future.

Jesus said to Peter, "Jesus said unto him, Verily I say unto thee, That this night, before the cock crow, thou shalt deny me thrice." (Luke 24:34). But the part I love is when He said, "when thou art converted strengthen the brethren" (Luke 22:32). Jesus in that statement declared his denial and his recommitment. In other words, I'm setting into motion, the necessities that will prevent you from staying in your sin. Before you've done foolishly, I've gone ahead and prepared your forgiveness and acceptance. Jesus revealed to Peter the knowledge of the near future and the not so near. The power of the spoken word is such, even with knowledge of the future, Peter could not prevent himself from denying Jesus. Alteration of the future was not allowed. Look at this:

> Now the next day that followed the day of the preparation, the chief priests and Pharisees came together unto Pilate, saying, 'Sir, we remember that that deceiver said, while he was yet alive, after three days I will rise again. Command therefore that the sepulcher be made sure until the third day, lest his disciples come by night, and steal him away, and say

unto the people, He is risen from the dead: so the last error shall be worse than the first.' Pilate said unto them, 'ye have a watch: go your way, make it as sure as ye can.' So they went, and made the sepulcher sure, sealing the stone, and setting a watch (Matthew 27:62-66).

Here is the war. Jesus uttered the words that He will rise again on the third day. Understand the words you speak have invited a war. But it's a war that your divine utterances cannot lose. Victory is certain. All the negative elements available are released against the prophetic declarations about you. But the words of God are actively fighting. As you partner with God and repeat these words, they act like reinforcements. A common mistake is to quit as the negatives are magnified, making the truth seem far and distant. But that's the enemy working overtime to get you to doubt and murmur. Full confidence must be employed to the Word of God. Come with me to Matthew 8:8-13.

The centurion answered and said, 'Lord, I am not worthy that thou shouldest come under my roof: but speak the word only, and my servant shall be healed. For I am a man under authority, having soldiers under me: and I say to this man, Go, and he goeth; and to another, Come, and he cometh; and to my servant, Do this, and he doeth it.' When Jesus heard it, he marvelled, and said to them that followed, 'Verily I say unto you, I have not found so great faith, no, not in Israel.' And Jesus said unto the centurion, 'Go thy way; and as thou hast believed, so be it done unto thee.'

And his servant was healed in the selfsame hour (Matthew 8:8-13).

Jesus did not go, He sent His words. This is a critical bit of information. Why? According to John 1, the word is Jesus. Therefore the word and Jesus are the same. So, when Jesus sends His word, it's as good as though Jesus was present.

What do we know about the word? The word knows your location. The word is equipped with all that is needed to secure your recovery/victory/turnaround. I beseech you brethren, by the mercies of God, that we begin to create our future as we speak in the present. As we renew our minds and invest in our future, let us please ensure that our words and actions are in sync. Practice what you preach and declare. If you declare you are more than a conqueror, then you must live as such. This was not a new concept that Jesus had coined, it existed long before He physically entered the scene. King David gave us a beautiful demonstration in 1 Samuel 17:45-47.

Then said David to the Philistine, Thou comest to me with a sword, and with a spear, and with a shield: but I come to thee in the name of the Lord of hosts, the God of the armies of Israel, whom thou hast defied. This day will the Lord deliver thee into mine hand, and I will smite thee, and take thine head from thee, and I will give the carcasses of the host of the Philistines this day unto the fowls of the air, and to the wild beasts of the earth; that all the earth may know that there is a God in Israel. And all this assembly shall know that the Lord saveth not with sword and spear: for the battle is the Lord's, and he will give you into our hands (1 Samuel 17:45-47).

Let me paraphrase what David said, "I come to you in the name of the LORD of hosts, and just in case you don't know who that is, He is the God of the army of Israel." David acknowledged and declared in whom his strength and victory lay. What he did, in essence, was to turn the battle over to God. Then he prophesied three things:

1. I will smite thee.
2. Remove thine head from thee.
3. Give thy carcasses to the fowls of the air and to a wild beast. (David then went back to the declaration.) When all this is done, God will be made known. Not I, David, but God.

What David did was to send his words in the name of the LORD, into his immediate future, to set in motion and create the victory needed. As we renew our minds, we must refrain from only being passive. There's a time and place for aggressive futuristic word-seeds to be planted. As we sow into our future, we must understand that different seeds have differing time frame before harvest is realized. Callaloo is known as a cash crop because it takes six weeks after planting to be harvested, while the Chinese bamboo, takes five years before anything is seen sprouting from the ground.

Depending on the situation in the present, you must choose wisely which seed you will plant. Wisdom guides you into not planting an untimely seed. In the time of crisis, an aggressive and quick seed is what you should implement. Pay attention. David did not go in his own strength, but in the name of the Lord. You should imitate David, declare in whose name your victory is and prophesy the outcome and then advance. Lest, you miss it, let's look at 1 Samuel 17: 48:

And it came to pass, when the Philistine arose, and came, and drew nigh to meet David, that David hasted, and ran toward the army to meet the Philistine (1 Samuel 17:48).

David partnered with his declared future. He ran towards the change he prophesied. Some have been declaring, prophesying but not partnering with their prophesied future. Having prophesied your season of marriage, it's now time to partner. You can partner by doing the following:

1. Invest in being the type of partner the Bible says your husband/wife deserves.
2. Start cleaning the junk from your emotional and psychological closet.
3. Get counseling for all unresolved issues
4. Examine financial status and repair where needed.
5. Make a list of the qualities you desire in your future husband/wife and pray about them.
6. Attend marriage seminars and conferences, buy books on intimacy.

7. Make your wedding list, and make possible colour theme after viewing many.

If you desire to own and operate your own motor vehicle, you need to learn to drive. Get your driver's license. You believe God has called you to travel the world in ministry, while you wait for the release, get your passport and apply to the embassies for visas.

Look at his attitude! He ran towards the giant. As we renew our minds, our attitude must also be transformed, which can mean being in a different place from the crowd which surrounds you. Prior to David's arrival, the soldiers of the army of Israel ran from Goliath, but David had a renewed mindset which propelled him to run towards the enemy. Physically they were in the same geographical location but perception transported him beyond their defeat to victory. The soldiers saw a mighty man of war, David envisioned a dead, headless uncircumcised Philistine. Like David, your victory begins in your perception and must be manifested in attitude and actions.

David was a man of his word! This is an area that we need to spend quality time developing. Letting our words be our bond. He made three promises to his enemy/situation and he delivered on his words as we see in 1 Samuel 17:51:

Therefore David ran, and stood upon the Philistine, and took his sword, and drew it out of the sheath thereof, and slew him, and cut off his head therewith (1 Samuel 17:51).

He kept his promise to a dead enemy. This is an excellent example of living what you preach. There is wealth unrealized in the utterances and actions of David. He told the enemy, "I'm going to cut off your head," without having a sword for himself. David taught us a powerful lesson. Not all that you will need to accomplish that which you desire, must necessarily be owned by you. Folly is the belief that any one person is self-sufficient. David told Goliath, in order for me to fulfil my promise to you, I will use your own resources. You will not be in a position to prevent me, so I'm just letting you know.

This emphasizes the need for partnership. As we renew our minds daily, we must take stock of what is available to us from the secrets of our enemies and utilize them to our advantage. Makes no sense to recreate the wheel. Scripture puts it nicely, "and the wealth of the sinner is laid up for the just" (Proverbs 13:22). We see the same sword being given to David as he fled from Saul who desired to kill him.

And David said unto Ahimelech, And is there not here under thine hand spear or sword? for I have neither brought my sword nor my weapons with me, because the king's business required haste. And the priest said, The sword of Goliath the Philistine, whom thou slewest in the valley of Elah, behold, it is here wrapped in a cloth behind the ephod: if thou wilt take that, take it: for there is no other save that here. And David said, There is none like that; give it me (1 Samuel 21:8-9).

Goliath's treasured sword awaited David. He took it once but now it's given to him. He said, there is none like it. This was no ordinary sword, it was designed for a champion. There is a constant fight to derail us from our assignments. Be resolute! Many persons are seeking a word from God. I have a question for you. What have you done with the last words you received from God? It's time to stop just allowing the wind to carry us. This is more than a good time of dancing and singing.

Let your words be an offensive weapon which function in a three-dimensional capacity. They cut, clear and plant. Visualize an overgrown plot of land, being attacked by your words. The bushes are first cut, the debris cleared and then the seeds of the desired results are planted. Your words are so powerful it attracts enemies. Notice when a prophetic Word is released, a countering fight commences. You say, "God, I was OK until the prophetic declarations." This is because there is a war in hot pursuit with the purpose of cancelling the effect of what was declared. For David, his overgrown plot of land was Goliath. You must identify your Goliath and release your words to cut, clear and plant.

Let us learn from all this, the importance of the choices we make. Daily you are gifted with the responsibility to sow word seeds to your detriment or your success. Remember, you are living today yesterday's choices, and tomorrow you will live today's decisions. Be conscious that your word-seeds today affect your tomorrow.

MIND RENEWAL KEYS

In this chapter on "The Word-Seed," we have shared some Mind Renewal keys to help you to become a better person. Here is a summary of these keys that you can apply to your life daily or as the circumstances arise. Read and meditate on them. Pray and declare them over your life to walk in the victory God has prepared for you.

1. Choose wisely that which is allowed to leave your mouth.
2. Understand that your words are so powerful, they can defile (mar, spoil) your future.
3. The word is equipped with all that is needed to secure your recovery/victory/turnaround.
4. You must refrain from only being passive. There's a time and place for aggressive futuristic word-seeds to be planted.
5. As you sow into your future, you must understand that different seeds have differing time frame before harvest is realized.

6. Your attitude must also be transformed, which can mean being in a different place from the crowd which surrounds you.
7. Let your words be your bond.
8. Not all you will need to accomplish that which you desire, must necessarily be owned by you.
9. Take stock of what is available to you from the secrets of your enemies and utilize them to your advantage.
10. You must identify your Goliath and release your words to cut, clear and plant.

CHAPTER 3:

PRAYING VS. COMMANDING

"Ignorance and incorrect application will find you dying of thirst although water supply is in abundance."
—Leostone Morrison

Both praying and commanding involve the spoken word. The difference is the order and tone in which they are delivered and the direction to which it proceeds. Prayers are directed to God while commands are done towards where change or obedience is required. God commands us to pray and to command. Prayer is requesting that God acts on your behalf while commanding is acting on your behalf based on the commands/authority of God. While prayer can be done internally (within your mind, spirit) command must be external (uttered or physically directed).

Hear this powerful truth as we renew our minds: we should not always pray. There are times when what is required is the act of command. In John 11: 41-42, Jesus prayed to God the Father. Jesus had no doubt that the Father heard Him. He was confident in that truth so He thanked His Father for hearing Him always. In prayer, you must adopt that principle, God hears you always. He is not deaf, asleep or too busy. Jesus expressed the benefits of prayer in John 14:13, "And whatsoever ye shall ask in my name, that will I do, that the Father may be glorified in the Son." Therefore, getting an answer from Him is not because of your quietness or shouting, but your asking in faith.

In John 11:43, Jesus said "Lazarus, come forth." That was not a prayer but a command. Jesus did not pray to the Father to send out Lazarus. He commanded the dead Lazarus to come forth. Is it remotely possible that you have not been seeing answered prayers because you prayed instead of commanding? Job 22:28 says, "Thou shalt also decree a thing, and it shall be established unto thee." In the biblical era, whenever a king decrees a thing it becomes life. It must take place and this is the privilege of us who have been adopted into the kinship of the King of Kings.

Whenever you command a word you must see it come to life. Romans 4:17 states, "calleth those things which be not as though they were." This is exercising the element of faith. Praying or commanding without faith will not yield any favorable results. The God you serve speaks and when He speaks elements give way to creation. In the creation account of Genesis, He spoke and everything came into being. We often times do not know the power that lies in our tongue and we make the mistake of speaking death instead of life. We have a creative tongue which can either create life or kill it. Whatever we send out in the atmosphere will take shape after a while.

> And when Jesus was entered into Capernaum, there came unto him a centurion, beseeching him, And saying, LORD, my servant lieth at home sick of the palsy, grievously tormented. And Jesus saith unto him, I will come and heal him. The centurion answered and said, LORD, I am not worthy that thou shouldest come under my roof: but speak the word only, and my servant shall be healed. For I am a man under authority, having soldiers under me: and I say to this man, Go, and he goeth; and to another, Come, and he cometh; and to my servant, Do this, and he doeth it. When Jesus heard it, he marvelled, and said to them that followed, Verily I say unto you, I have not found so great faith, no, not in Israel. And Jesus said unto the centurion, Go thy way; and as thou hast believed, so be it done unto thee. And his servant was healed in the selfsame hour (Matthew 8:5-10,13).

A centurion is the commander of a century (100) soldiers in the ancient Roman army.

What marveled Jesus was the man's faith. Where was his faith demonstrated? It was in his understanding of authority. Being a military man, he understood that those who are under his authority must obey his command. This he expressed to Jesus. He will not ask one to come or go, rather he commands them to go or come. The centurion tapped into a realm that caused Jesus to marvel. He tapped into who Jesus was. He got the revelation that Jesus was above (has authority over) all sickness and geography.

Jesus having authority over geography needed not to be in the same location, because all space is one to Him. Hence the centurion said, "You don't need to come to my house, just speak the word." The spoken word under the authority of Jesus is equipped with a precise navigational system. It knows where to locate you. The centurion also understood that Jesus' words were a replica of himself. If the word is sent, Jesus is sent. Jesus and His words are one.

What does this mean for us as children of the King? Luke 10:19 says, "Behold, I give unto you power to tread on serpents and scorpions, and over all the power of the enemy: and nothing shall by any means hurt you." Then in Mark 16, Jesus told the disciples that he had given them authority in His name. As we renew our minds, be it known that Jesus will not do for you what He has given you the authority to do. You have authority to cast out devils, to heal the sick and speak in new tongues and drink deadly poison without being hurt. Stop praying asking Jesus to get the evil spirits out of your house. Use that God-given authority and command in the name of Jesus.

When I attended the International Accelerated Missions Bible School, I witnessed an encounter where the power of command was demonstrated. The class had finished but we were prevented from getting to the parking lot because of a heavy downpour of rain. One teacher, Prophetess Stamp, stood at the doorway, raised her hands to the heavens and commanded the rain to cease and instantly the rain stopped. At the beginning of November 2018, the church planned to do a community prayer walk, then came the rain. I remembered to command and exercise my faith and the clouds obeyed my command. Renew your mind by using your God-given authority to command. You're a person of authority, stop acting like a wimp.

Take authority over your finances, health, home and the atmosphere. Hear what Philippians tells us in chapter 2:10, "Wherefore God also hath highly exalted him, and given him a name which is above every name: that at the name of Jesus every knee should bow, of things in heaven, and things in earth, and things under the earth..." You see the same sentiments being echoed to Peter as Jesus encourages him not to limit himself to operating only in the physical realm. "And I will give unto thee the keys of the kingdom of heaven: and whatsoever thou shalt bind on earth shall be bound in heaven: and whatsoever thou shalt loose on earth shall be loosed in heaven" (Matthew 16:19).

Renew your mind with this; when Jesus said He has given us authority in His name, we were not given limited power. Our authority transcends heavens, earth and under the earth. We command our victory on every battleground. You're not expected to lose some and win some.

And when he saw a fig tree in the way, he came to it, and found nothing thereon, but leaves only, and said unto it, Let no fruit grow on thee henceforward forever. And presently the fig tree withered away. And when the disciples saw it, they marvelled, saying, How soon is the fig tree withered away! Jesus answered and said unto them, Verily I say unto you, If ye have faith, and doubt not, ye shall not only do this which is done to the fig tree, but also if ye shall say unto this mountain, Be thou removed, and be thou cast into the sea; it shall be done (Matthew 21:19-21).

Fig trees take between 2-5 years before they are mature enough to produce figs. Why is this important? There are situations that have been running years now and it's time for us to command in the name of Jesus Christ, that they dry up from the root. Stop praying about it, command it to cease.

Jesus marveled when the centurion told him to command the healing of his sick servant. Now the disciples marvel at Jesus' command and the effect of that command to the fig tree.

Jesus commanded the tree to die. On another occasion, Jesus commanded the wind and the waves to be still. Do wind, sea, and trees have ears?

Remember the story of Lazarus mentioned earlier. Pay attention, Jesus did not say come alive, He called him out of the grave. Jesus said, "Lazarus, come forth." Upon the announcement of his name, he that was dead responded and then came forth. Jesus said come forth without seeing if Lazarus had responded to his name. That's confidence in one's authority and power. You cannot command doubtingly nor can you wait to see step one fulfilled before commanding step two. Command and believe by faith that it's done.

Having the same authority as Jesus, you must understand that you live in the physical realm yet have the authority and power to affect the spirit realm. Your commands transcend realms. Remember what Jesus said, if you have faith as small as a mustard seed you shall not only speak to fig trees but mountains. A command without faith is madness. Faith must be the engine. That is the driving force that sets into motion things prayed for or commanded. Remember without faith it is impossible to please God.

There is a difference between authority and power. In government, the term authority is often used interchangeably with power. However, their meanings differ. While power is defined as "the ability to influence somebody to do something that he/she would not have done" (*Black's Law Dictionary*, Torts; Prosser, Wade, and Schwartz's, 12 Ed), authority is the legal and formal right to give orders and commands, and take decisions (Key Differences, 2016). As you synchronize your mind to the complete will of God, embrace this truth: you have been entrusted with both power and the legal authority to utilize that power. This power and authority must be demonstrated through praying and commanding.

You have been given the necessary tools of praying and commanding to be used in securing the already won victory. However, ignorance and incorrect application will find you dying of thirst although water supply is in abundance. Some things you ask for, some you command. You will ask God for knowledge of His will, or interpretation of a dream but you command demons and command sickness out and away.

Some years ago, I attended an all-night prayer meeting at a church. Upon arrival, I heard the Holy Spirit say, "Observe." During the session, evil spirits manifested within a young man which caused him to be acting and speaking nonsensically. The leaders of the meeting, anointed him with oil, prayed and sang songs of healing and deliverance, but to no avail. This dragged on painfully until a command was given to the evil spirits in the name of Jesus Christ.

Many persons are waiting for an answer to earnestly prayed prayers, and God is waiting for them to utilize what He has bestowed upon them. Therefore, stop waiting on Jesus to do for you what He has already given you the authority to do. He never said if you have mustard seed faith He will move your mountains, but if you have it, you shall move them. Renewing your mind to the will of God must pull you to develop two essential cultures: praying and commanding. These should become your new lifestyle. Please, decipher, when it's praying time versus commanding time. Your victory awaits you.

MIND RENEWAL KEYS

In this chapter on "Commanding vs. Praying" we have shared some Mind Renewal keys to help you to become a better person. Here is a summary of these keys that you can apply to your life daily or as the circumstances arise. Read and meditate on them. Pray and declare them over your life to walk in the victory God has prepared for you.

1. When Jesus said He has given us authority in His name, we were not given limited power. Our authority transcends heavens, earth and under the earth.
2. Use your God-given authority to command. You're a person of authority.
3. The spoken word under the authority of Jesus is equipped with a precise navigational system. It knows where to locate you.
4. Jesus will not do for you what He has given you the authority to do.
5. A command without faith is madness. Don't wait to see step one fulfilled before commanding step two.

CHAPTER 4:

THE PROMISED WORD

"Use the promise of God as your cushion and pillow through the between periods." —Leostone Morrison

I lost a dear friend of mine because I made a promise and did not fulfil it. At the time, I couldn't understand why she was so hurt by me not fulfilling the small promise I made. I told her, I would call her back and didn't. As the children of Israel left Egypt, God promised to give them land for themselves. Moses sent twelve (12) spies to search the land, ten (10) returned with bad reports but Caleb and Joshua had good reports. The emphasis here is on Caleb.

And the Lord heard the voice of your words, and was wroth, and sware, saying, Surely there shall not one of these men of this evil generation see that good land, which I sware to give unto your fathers, save Caleb the son of Jephunneh; he shall see it, and to him will I give the land that he hath trodden upon, and to his children, because he hath wholly followed the Lord (Deuteronomy 1:34-36).

Caleb had a promise. He would cross over into the Promised Land, the very land that he walked on and spied out would be given to him.

According to the Merriam Webster's dictionary, a promise is "a legally binding declaration that gives the person to whom it is made a right to expect or to claim the performance or forbearance of a specified act." Caleb held to this promise and forty-five years later, went to Joshua to claim his inheritance.

And Moses sware on that day, saying, Surely the land whereon thy feet have trodden shall be thine inherit-ance, and thy children's forever, because thou hast wholly followed the Lord my God. And now, behold, the Lord hath kept me alive, as he said, these forty and five years, even since the Lord spake this word unto Moses, while the children of Israel wandered in the wilderness: and now, lo, I am this day fourscore and five years old. As yet I am as strong this day as I was in the day that Moses sent me: as my strength was then, even so is my strength now, for war, both to go out, and to come in. Now therefore give me this mountain, whereof the Lord spake in that day; for thou heardest in that day how the Anakims were there, and that the cities were great and fenced: if so be the Lord will be with me, then I shall be able to drive them out, as the Lord said (Joshua 14:9-12).

Caleb tapped into a realm where the promised word stands as established truth. When this promise was made to Caleb, a seed was planted. For forty-five years he nurtured it with faith and confidence knowing that once God speaks it, then that's it. It's settled. Hear what Philippians 1:6 says, "being confident of this very thing, that he which hath begun a good work in you will perform it until the day of Jesus Christ."

This great work began by way of a promise. Caleb had all legal and spiritual rights to claim his promise. Why? As we renew our minds, we are forced to recognize that a promise is not just words but within the spirit realm, the land was transferred. When Caleb said, "Give me this mountain that was promised to me," he was in essence saying, I have had this transfer in the spirit realm, now it's time for it to be made manifest in the physical realm. I have the spiritual deed, now I need the physical.

Ownership does not mean occupation. He owned the land but it was occupied by another. Basically, they were tending to his land. They were caretakers. The sad truth is, they did not know it. There are some wealth that has been delivered into our spirit by the Holy Spirit, and it's time for us like Caleb, to demand what is rightfully ours.

We will remember David, he was anointed as King over Israel but Saul remained on the throne. Saul occupied David's throne and position for twenty years after his anointing. The transfer was done. God had rejected Saul but still allowed him to work. A miserable reality is that you can be engaged on an assignment for which you do not have the anointing. This results in work and not the fulfilment of one's calling. A man's calling is not a chore, task but his passion and life. Are you living or existing, are you working or fulfilling?

Unfortunately, because a few years have passed, and we have not seen a fulfilment of those promises, we bury them in the miscellaneous file. You must begin to live from a renewed mind where the principle of God is adopted. God says we are to "let our yeah be yeah and our nays be nay" (Matt. 5:37). With our minds renewed, we are now in partnership with the Holy Spirit to bring back to remembrance every already established truth (promise) that He God has made unto us.

WORK THE PROMISE

The Shunammite woman who was childless received a prophetic word that she would bring forth a child. She received the promise and despite the odds against her husband (he was old), she understood that he is the only promise helper that must be employed. In other words, the promise did not give her the right to step out of the covenant because the covenant had issues. Challenges are not licenses to do it your way. God's way must be and remain the only way.

It's in the pursuit of doing it God's way we encounter the miracle as we take the step. The period between the promise and the manifestation is critical. This is where a lot of dreams get aborted. Many persons get lost in "The Between" because they try to help God. That's evidence of wavering and doubting the Almighty God. A dear friend of mine saw visions of herself doing ministry. Huge masses of people followed her, desiring to hear the word of God. In her period of The Between, she got involved with a guy. Left the faith and got a baby. She is presently finding her way back home.

Did you hear the celebration? We rejoiced with brother and sister Brown on this their fortieth wedding anniversary. The church rejoiced and the Browns hugged. That is the wedding date—40th anniversary. *The Between* is not spoken. The days of not speaking to each other, no intimacy, cheating, outside children, monies spent without consent, nights of fasting, fights with in-laws. And the list goes on. That is what is called "The In Between." The Shunamite woman perhaps asked herself:

How do I approach my husband? Will he think I'm seeking to humiliate him, knowing his limitations? Do I tell him the word from the man of God? If I do, will he question what was I doing at his quarters or do I just go in unto him and trust God to have His way? Should I make my move early in the morning after he awakens or in the evening after he is pleased with the day's work? Should I call some prayer warriors to pray me through or should I sow seed into the ministry? I know, forget this! The man of God means well but he is mistaken. I think he saw a baby but it's Gehazi's own. Oh man of God must be tired. How can I make his room more comfortable?

In the above, the thoughts started from a place of hope, optimism and plummeted to a shift—a dangerous shift.

Let us renew our minds in this direction. The fountain connected to your purpose will flow again. Push through your "The Between." Stay in the will of God. Cry if you have to, bawl if you must, but don't commit promise suicide. Take the Step. REFUSE the temptation to abandon the promise of God. Let it become your daily recital. Put in what He has promised you and say the following, "I know what the situation looks like, but God promised me." Never lose hope of God's truth. Use the promise of God as your cushion and pillow through "The Between" periods.

Years ago, my mother was seriously out of money and she would go to the bus stop without bus fare. The Lord made a promise to her by way of a dream. She saw herself driving a beautiful car. Of course, the faithful God delivered on His promise. After fifteen (15) years, she purchased a lovely Silver Honda Stream seven-seater car. During the seemingly long *in-between period*, she learned to drive, saved and prepared her drive way. God provided the means to make the promise a fulfilment. God is our chief partner.

MIND RENEWAL KEYS

In this chapter on "The Promised Word" we have shared some Mind Renewal keys to help you to become a better person. Here is a summary of these keys that you can apply to your life daily or as the circumstances arise. Read and meditate on them. Pray and declare them over your life to walk in the victory God has prepared for you.

1. The promised word is established truth.
2. Assignment without the anointing is work and not the fulfilment of one's calling.
3. Challenges are not license to do it your way. God's way must be and remain the only way. It's in the pursuit of doing it God's way that we encounter the miracle as we take the step.
4. The fountain connected to your purpose will flow again. Push through your "Between."

Chapter 5:

Great Spirits and

Mediocre Minds

Great spirits have always encountered violent opposition from mediocre *minds.* Not everything that can be counted counts, and not everything that counts can be counted. Everybody is a genius. But if you judge a fish by its ability to climb a tree, it will live its whole life believing that it is stupid.

—Albert Einstein

The idea that "Great spirits have always encountered violent opposition from mediocre minds" is very thought provoking and true. One distinction between a great and a mediocre mind is their source of empowerment and direction. The Bible tells us "As a man thinketh in his heart, so is he" (Proverbs 23:7). Here lies the problem. We have not stretched our minds to inhabit high frequencies but have settled at low grounds. Recently I scanned the radio for channels but was disappointed with what the AM frequency offered. I switched over to the FM frequency which afforded me a greater variety. You will never tread the paths your mind has not gone. Your spirit acts as a forerunner. It goes into the spirit realm and navigates beyond physical boundaries through the process of thinking. The routes that need to be pursued are explored and decided on. There is another dimension of the forerunner which will be addressed in the section that deals with vision and sight.

In construction, the larger the building, the deeper the foundation must be, and so it is with the mind. The deeper the thoughts...the greater the rewards. A mediocre mind is one that has settled by refusing to expand its borders. In 2018, I listened to an invited speaker whose address highlighted the mind of the founder. He said, "The size of your auditorium (100-seater) expresses where your spirit took you, as you planned and executed your vision."

The journey of your spirit determines the height and depth of your expectations. The founder was not allowed to go beyond a hundred (100) seats because that's where his spirit stopped. All seats occupied meant a fruitful event but not necessarily a successful host. Achievement below your true potential is failure. Motivational speaker Les Brown says, "Most people fail in life not because they aim too high and miss, but because they aim too low and hit." As expansion and expectation take place in your spirit, there must be a matching expansion and expectation in your physical domain. This is to facilitate the increase. Two friends had a conversation. One said, "I'm going to work for my slice of the cake," the other responded, "why only a slice, why not work to own the bakery?" As you renew your mind, don't settle, expand the terrains of your mind and spirit.

Truth be told, there are great minds that have come and gone without ever realizing they were great. If we look at the education system, for the most part, everyone is tested and determined by the same measuring rod. Therefore, a fish will die believing it was stupid because it was not able to climb. You do the reverse and give a swimming exam, the fish does very well. The caterpillar would never know that in him lies a butterfly waiting to fly if he is in the wrong environment. An unrealized truth is, the greatest environment you need is not the one where your physical boots are accustomed to, but the one where your spirit trods daily within your minds. What is the state of your mental environment? A wealthy spirit will prosper where mediocre minds perish; same terrain but different results. As you renew your minds, refuse to be a victim of an impoverished environment but rather let the journey of your Great Spirit foster global changes.

Mediocre minds refuse to evolve and grow through constant mind renewal. Rather than learning to fly across the open fields, they crawl among petals of green. The word of God encourages us to declare those things that are not as though they are (Romans 4:17). It says, "let the weak say I am strong" (Joel 3:10). Is the sacred book encouraging persons to lie? No. It is an encouragement to not reside at the place of your handicap. While your experience is that of need, see yourself in plenty. This will then become your goal to move forward.

When I first began receiving in my spirit ideas for books and songs, although strapped for money, I made a covenant with God. I will give away twenty five per-cent (25%) of all revenues received from sales of these materials. The physical environment shouted loudly, you are broke, but my spirit travelled to a place of abundance. You need to pursue synchronization between your spirit man's truth and your physical manifestations. Your evolving or expanding mind must always attract and pull your physical domain to the manifestation of more. Let's listen to a great mind speak on the heels of injustice towards the black man.

I have a dream that one day on the red hills of Geor-gia, the sons of former slaves and the sons of former slave owners will be able to sit down together at the table of brotherhood.

I have a dream that one day even the state of Missis-sippi, a state sweltering with the heat of injustice, sweltering with the heat of oppression, will be trans-formed into an oasis of freedom and justice.

I have a dream that my four little children will one day live in a nation where they will not be judged by the colour of their skin but by the content of their character.

I have a dream that one day down in Alabama, with its vicious racists, with its governor having his lips dripping with the words of "interposition" and "nulli-fication" (Yes), one day right there in Alabama little black boys and black girls will be able to join hands with little white boys and white girls as sisters and brothers. I have a dream today.

I have a dream that one day every valley shall be exalted, every hill and mountain shall be made low, the rough places will be made plain, and the crooked places will be made straight, and the glory of the Lord shall be revealed, and all flesh shall see it together.

This is our hope. This is the faith that I go back to the South with. With this faith, we will be able to hew out of the mountain of despair a stone of hope. With this faith, we will be able to transform the jangling discords of our nation into a beautiful symphony of brotherhood. With this faith, we will be able to work together, to pray together, to struggle together, to go to jail together, to stand up for freedom together knowing that we will be free one day (Martin Luther King Jr.).

The above is an excerpt from Martin Luther King Jr.'s famous speech, which he delivered on August 28, 1963, at the Southern Christian Leadership Conference held in Washington, D.C. King spoke from two places, the mediocre and the great. The mediocre had accepted a system where one race believed it was superior to another, but King's great mind refused to accept such an inhumane and repulsive belief. He spoke of change. A change where all men are treated as created from the same mind—the mind of God. Great minds are not afraid to go against the system of injustice, even if it cost them their earthly lives. This was true in King's case. King was assassinated on April 4, 1968.

In 2017, I heard a guest speaker at a conference say, "he wants to go the grave empty." At first glance I thought, "That's nothing deep, as we all go to the grave empty." However, as he expounded, I realized he spoke of emptying his great mind in service to the Lord and his fellow humans. How many persons have contributed to making the cemetery the wealthiest place on earth? They died with books, movies, poems, business ventures, ministries, and other world-changing ideas that remained locked up in their minds.

The truth is, a great mind functions like a motor vehicle alternator. The alternator is a creator of electric power in your car and is a chief component of a vehicle's charging system. Each time the engine is in motion, the alternator charges the battery and supplies added electric power for the vehicle's electrical systems. If the alternator is not working, the vehicle's power is solely on the battery which is not being recharged. That battery will eventually run out of juice and die. I believe this is how the mind functions. Activating our minds towards purpose intentionally requires a high frequency which serves as a recharging methodology. As you release your God given deposits, be it businesses, books, movies or multimillion dollar ideas, you will be rejuvenated or replenished. The more you release, the more you will receive to continue giving. A great mind will always have and desire to give of its reservoir.

The idea of going to the grave empty and its implications have stirred up much controversy. According to 2 Kings 13:21 "And it came to pass, as they were burying a man, that, behold, they spied a band of men; and they cast the man into the sepulcher of Elisha: and when the man was let down and touched the bones of Elisha, he revived, and stood up on his feet." This is the only place in the Bible this is seen. It is believed that Elisha's protégé Gehazi sinned and was stripped of his spiritual inheritance. Therefore, Elisha unlike his mentor Elijah, who passed on the mantle to him the day he was transported into heaven, did not transfer his anointing before his death. Although Elisha died, the anointing was still alive in his bones, hence the resurrection of the dead.

In 2015, students of New Bethel Church in Redding California went to the graves of anointed men and women of God, doing what is called "grave sucking." This practice saw persons lying on the graves and seeking the anointing of the deceased. Erroneously, they sought from the dead what was afforded by the living Holy Spirit. There is a danger of commencing great but ending foolishly. The folks from Bethel Church had an excellent, great desire. They decided to pursue that endeavour. They wanted to receive the anointing and function in the power of the demonstrated anointing of the great fathers of the faith.

However, their poverty-stricken frame of mind caused them to collapse into the occult. The route they should have chosen is embracing the truth in the word of God. "But you will receive power when the Holy Spirit comes on you, and you will be my witnesses in Jerusalem, and in all Judea and Samaria, and to the ends of the earth" (Acts 1:8). They were not obeying the undiluted word of God. One of the marks of a wealthy mind is its willingness to obey and live the undiluted word of God.

A poor or unhealthy mind will always seek and promote the wrong source. In 1994, someone used witchcraft against me by using my Certificate Mathematics textbook. I was confined to the University Hospital for nine days. A distant family member, who meant well encouraged my mother (who is a Christian) to go to an obeah man for help. Her response was, "if God chooses not to heal him, then so be it. But I'm not dirtying my hands with iniquity." We can see two minds conversing: a poor mind and a rich mind. The poor mind refused the high standard of God that warns us to avoid persons who consult the dead, mediums and any agent of Satan. The rich or empowered mind resides at the place where the knowledge of God is sovereign. A rich or empowered mind will choose to do what God desires and obtains a place of rest.

Your educational matriculation, wealth acquisition or societal status does not necessarily represent the state of your mind. Nor is it determined by the poverty of your comrades. Your great or mediocre spirit rests on your willingness to pursue daily mind renewal, which is achieved primarily through the word of God. The throne of your submission speaks volumes to the state of your spirit. Rejection or acceptance of God's words is a mighty mind renewal measuring scale. As you renew your mind, it is imperative that the word of God becomes your bench mark. Once your great spirit moves in line with the word of God, it stays actively involved as the forerunner. Mediocrity and stagnation therefore can no longer cross the borders of a renewed mind; instead, expectancy and expansion become the new normal.

MIND RENEWAL KEYS

In this chapter on "Great Spirits and Mediocre Minds" we have shared some Mind Renewal keys to help you to become a better person. Here is a summary of these keys that you can apply to your life daily or as the circumstances arise. Read and meditate on them. Pray and declare them over your life to walk in the victory God has prepared for you.

1. Achievement below your true potential is failure.
2. You will never tread the paths your mind has not gone.
3. We have not stretched our minds to inhabit high frequencies but have settled at low grounds.
4. A wealthy spirit will prosper where mediocre minds perish.
5. Mediocre minds refuse to evolve and grow through constant mind renewal. Rather than learning to fly across the open fields, they crawl among petals of green.
6. Reject low grounds and stretch your mind to inhabit high frequencies.

7. As expansion and expectation take place in your spirit, there must be a matching expansion and expectation in your physical domain.

8. An unrealized truth is that the greatest environment you need is not the one where your physical boots are accustomed to, but the one where your spirit trods daily within your mind.

9. Great minds are not afraid to go against the system of injustice, even if it costs them their earthly lives.

10. Activating your minds towards purpose intentionally requires a high frequency, which serves as a recharging methodology.

11. A great mind will always have and desire to give of its reservoir.

12. A poor or unhealthy mind will always seek and promote the wrong source.

13. Let the word of God be your bench mark.

Chapter 6:

Perspective and Mind Renewal

"I freed a thousand slaves. I could have freed a thousand more if only they knew they were slaves."

—Harriet Tubman

In a recent post on social media, a young man said he was engaged in a conversation with a seemingly insane man. The man said to him, "Am I mad because I see things differently from others?" To this, he replied "no." The man then drew the letter "M" on a piece of paper and asked him what it was. He replied, "M." The seemingly madman responded, "It depends on the angle from which you are looking. If you turn it over, you see W, turn it to the right you get a three, and if you turn it to the left, you have an E." He ended the dialogue by saying, "he is not mad because he sees things differently."

What was highlighted was perceptions are arrived at based on the angle from which we are looking. So, is the glass half full or is it half empty? The truth of the matter is: it's both. However, the path chosen will be dependent upon one's perception.

Some years ago, a doctor asked me to befriend a young man who had no friends. I agreed and took the challenge. From our few conversations, I remember distinctly this one. The young man said, "he was able to stand in the rain, uncovered and not get wet." I immediately categorized him as one who is mentally unstable. Years later, as my mind expanded, I pondered his statement and I realized, he was more stable than I thought. I now understand and agree with his perception. Human beings are called "tripartite beings," meaning three parts.

According to 1 Thessalonians 5:23 "And the very God of peace sanctify you wholly; and I pray God your whole spirit and soul and body be preserved blameless unto the coming of our Lord Jesus Christ." This indicates that human beings are body, soul and spirit. Let's briefly expound on the function of each part for you to see what the young man was trying to convey:

1. Your body is the visible component of man which communicates in the physical domain through its five senses.
2. The Greek word for soul in the Bible is *psyche*, which is also the word of origin for psychology. You have knowledge and experience of the psychological realm through your soul. Your soul is who you are from an internal perspective and

is a combination of your mind, emotions and your will. The mind facilitates thoughts, memory and reasoning. Your emotions allow you to have feelings like joy or sorrow and your will, enables you to make decisions.

3. Your spirit is the most sacred part of your existence. Through your spirit, you connect with the spiritual realm. God is a spirit, therefore your highest level of communication with Him, is channeled through this component.

We have predominantly in ignorance only focused on the body which amounts to 1/3 of who we are. The young man spoke from the perspective of his body being wet but not his soul (mind) and his spirit. He reasoned that the greater portion of his existence which is 2/3, being soul and spirit were not affected by that which was affecting the external (the rain). He saw the lopsided discrepancy of humans focusing on the body while neglecting the internal soul and spirit.

Daily you wash, groom, clothe, perfume and rest your bodies, but how much time do you allocate for the soul and spirit? Hear this perspective! You have been confined to the physical realm when the spiritual realm awaits you with embracing arms. To receive the victories you long for will require you to shift your focus and place the spirit realm above the physical. You must pay more attention to your soul and spirit. The young man spoke in his simple way: we must not be consumed by the externals which have the potential to bully us into succumbing to their dictates. Galatians 5: 16-17 puts it this way:

This I say then, Walk in the Spirit, and ye shall not fulfil the lust of the flesh. For the flesh lusteth against the Spirit, and the Spirit against the flesh: and these are contrary the one to the other: so that ye cannot do the things that ye would (Galatians 5:16-17).

There is a continuous war within the tripartite creation of man. It's between the body and the spirit. A victorious life is one that has yielded not to the body but to the spirit. This young man had tapped into an understanding that professed great minds have yet to grasp. The late Bob Marley said, "Some people feel the rain. Others just get wet." Here he spoke on two fronts, the mind (feelings) and body (get wet). An arresting truth is many persons live their lives only experiencing the wetness but never feeling the rain. When an encounter ministers to your mind, and soul, then the process of mind renewal can start or continue.

The great Nelson Mandela said it this way: "As I walked out the door toward the gate that would lead to my freedom, I knew if I didn't leave my bitterness and hatred behind, I'd still be in prison." He spoke a truth that submerged beneath the shell of the human body. Though freed from the bars of physical confinement, continued imprisonment would remain a reality, if he were not mentally and spiritually free. These are the subtle and easily overlooked chains. Mandela mentioned bitterness and hatred as bars and chains of mental captivity, but the chain has many links. Un-forgiveness, low self-esteem, fear, past failures, regret, and abuse are some links of the chain that holds us captive.

When you mature to the place of being spiritually wealthy, physical bars are unable to restrain you. Your best movies, songs, books, and poetry can be written in a place of physical and earthly restraint. What is imperative is the state of your mind, which though private, is manifested through your speech and deeds. The greater imprisonment is that of the mind and the spirit, where one is physically free, but spiritually bound. A parked spirit is like a sun without its light. There are more incarcerated persons roaming the streets than those in maximum security facilities. The irony is they are not aware that they are bound.

Harriet Tubman said: "I freed a thousand slaves. I could have freed a thousand more if only they knew they were slaves." They did not know because their feet and hands were unshackled. Robert Nesta (Bob) Marley in his musical hit, "Redemption Song" popularized these words first uttered by Marcus Garvey. "We are going to emancipate ourselves from mental slavery because whilst others might free the body, none but ourselves can free the mind." Until a man's mind is free, he may be loose externally but bound internally. Notice, Garvey levied the responsibility of mental emancipation upon individuals and not a system. You and I have to take up the mandate of our own Mind Renewal.

Let's look at two of the disciples of Jesus who were beaten and then imprisoned to see how important perspective and mind renewal are.

And when they had laid many stripes upon them, they cast them into prison, charging the jailor to keep them safely: Who, having received such a charge, thrust them into the inner prison, and made their feet fast in the stocks. And at midnight Paul and Silas prayed, and sang praises unto God: and the prisoners heard them. And suddenly there was a great earthquake, so that the foundations of the prison were shaken: and immediately all the doors were opened, and every one's bands were loosed (Acts 16:23-26).

Paul and Silas demonstrated this very life changing, Mind Renewal concept. Despite being physically abused through flogging and incarceration, their expressions of spiritual freedom stood as a testimony to the other prisoners. All were imprisoned but not all were bound. Just because we share the same space does not mean we are identical in our consciousness. They were singing unto God after just being beaten and imprisoned for God! As we renew our minds, let it resonate in our spirits that, an attack against your belief should serve to strengthen it and not cause a departure.

That which is of little or no value tends to be ignored. The physical pain from the beating had to surrender its voice to the overwhelming sound of their spirits as concerted worship was echoed. The choice was clear: "when in Rome do as the Romans do," which in this case was: "when in prison, do as the other prisoners do." Or be transported from the realm of pain and shame to a place of peace, joy, and worship. They found this new realm of peace, joy and worship through the spirit and soul. The Mind Renewal these two imprisoned men modeled was so powerful, that the other prisoners benefitted from their spiritual freedom. Their spiritual freedom impacted the physical realm. When you demonstrate the renewed mind's perspectives, others around you will be impacted positively. That's the power of a renewed mind. Persons who come in contact with you, are now positioned for change.

Spiritual and mental emancipation result in physical freedom. True faith is not at its best under peace but during the time of spiritual and physical unrest. Do we hold true to our faith under pressure? Or do we allow the physical chains to silence our praise? As you renew your minds, flee low level perspectives which are derived from bodily or physical experiences. Embrace perspectives that are directly attributed to your spiritual communication with your God and mental emancipation. An excellent place to start is, "And we know that ALL things work together for good to those who love God, to those who are the called according to His purpose" (Romans 8:28).

MIND RENEWAL KEYS

In this chapter on "Perspective and Mind Renewal" we have shared some Mind Renewal keys to help you to become a better person. Here is a summary of these keys that you can apply to your life daily or as the circumstances arise. Read and meditate on them. Pray and declare them over your life to walk in the victory God has prepared for you.

1. To receive the victories you long for will require you to shift your focus and place the spirit realm above the physical realm.
2. You must not be consumed by the externals which have the potential to bully us into succumbing to their dictates.
3. A victorious life is one that has yielded not to the body but to the spirit.
4. When you mature to the place of being spiritually wealthy, physical bars are unable to restrain you.
5. The greater imprisonment is that of the mind and the spirit, where one is physically free, but spiritually bound.
6. A parked spirit is like a sun without its light.
7. Let it resonate in our spirits that, an attack against your belief should serve to strengthen it and not cause a departure.
8. When you demonstrate the renewed mind's perspectives, others around you will be impacted positively.

CHAPTER 7:

CRACKED PERFORMERS

"Your cracks are not errors but rather the platform from which your extraordinary projects and influence can impact generations and nations."

—Leostone Morrison

According to Rhetoric and Writing at the College Level, "an angle of vision indicates that the author manipulates a message and how it gets across to the readers. We could easily say that an angle of vision is the author's point of view." The following is an ancient fable with much truth where several angles are examined.

An elderly Chinese woman had two large pots. Each pot hung on the ends of a pole, which she carried across her shoulders. Every day, she used this device to carry water to her home. One of the pots was perfect and always delivered a full portion of water. The other had a deep crack in it and leaked. At the end of the long walk from the stream to the house, the cracked pot arrived only half full.

For a full two years, this situation occurred daily, with the woman bringing home only one and a half pots of water. Of course, the perfect pot was proud of its accomplishments. But the poor cracked pot was ashamed of its own imperfection and miserable that it could only do half of what it had been made to do.

After two years of what it *perceived* to be bitter failure, the cracked pot spoke to the woman one day by the stream, saying, "I am ashamed of myself because this crack in my side causes water to leak out all the way back to your house."

The old woman smiled and replied, "Did you notice that there are flowers on your side of the path, but not on the other pot's side? I have always known about your flaw, so I planted flower seeds on your side of the path, and every day while we walked back home you watered them and made them grow. For two years, I have been able to pick these beautiful flowers to decorate the table and give to my friends and neighbours. Without you being just the way you are, there would not have been this special beauty to grace our homes and lives."

Sometimes, it's the "cracks," or what we perceive as imperfections, in this reality that create something unexpected and beautiful. These "cracks" allow something to change and ultimately make the whole much richer and more interesting. Everything and every being has its own unique purpose and destiny to fulfil.

What determines a person's point of view or angle of vision, are both external and internal factors such as our mind and emotions that make up our soul, which is our personality, which speaks to who we are within. External factors are bountiful. For the broken pot, the externals that impacted its perception of self were comparison and falling below the expectations of its design. This caused him to become ashamed and miserable (internal factor).

To excavate the wealth of this short story, we need to delve into the unspoken which can be derived from the spoken. We will explore the following perspectives:

a) The unbroken pot
b) The old lady
c) The decorated side of the road
d) The house
e) The neighbours
f) The flawed/cracked pot.

THE UNBROKEN POT

This perfect pot had all rights to be proud of its accomplishments. For two long years, it had faithfully served with excellence the purpose for which it was made. This is remarkable and should not be overlooked. Whenever persons serve faithfully they should be recognized both privately and publicly. It was reliable. The old lady could depend on it to deliver. It was money well spent.

THE OLD LADY

The nameless old lady had a situation. She needed to make a decision to move forward. The options before her were: discard the broken pot, mend it, use it to plant flowers or use it as it was. Her position can be likened to those who find themselves in difficult marriages. They too have similar options. Some choose to discard their marriage. Many marriages have hastily flatlined at divorce because of cracks that seemed humongous and beyond any sensible value. There is an unwillingness to pursue the vow of "until death do us part." Consequently, broken pots/relationships are no longer sacred.

The old lady and the pot had a relationship. She remembered the good times. The pot served well and added value to her life before it became cracked. She refused to leave the wounded behind. She knew it still had value although cracked, so she decided not to discard it or mend it.

Mending would be the next viable option if the old lady did not want to discard the pot but she chose not to. Why did she choose this option? I believe the associated cost, time and effort needed to restore the pot to its truest form would be too much. She could have used it to plant flowers. That could have worked because at least it would still be useful and producing quality service. She decided to preserve the dignity of their relationship. The pot/relationship was broken but not dead.

The old lady acknowledged the difference between her two pots. She refused to judge the broken pot on the basis of its flaw. She, through wisdom, capitalized on its brokenness and restored it to a place of value. In appreciating the condition or state of the broken pot, she expanded its horizon or area of service. The perfect water pot only served the old lady while, the broken pot served the community, her house, and her neighbours.

You must, therefore, understand that your broken-ness might just be your launching pad into unimaginable service. The old lady loved both pots with their differences. She needed the water for her household necessities and depended on the perfect pot to deliver that service rather than the broken pot. Therefore, you must stop expecting more than we know others are able to deliver. Did you notice that the old lady never argued with the flawed pot about its inability to deliver in the same manner as its counterpart? In this way she demonstrated that vision is more powerful than sight.

Sight saw the cracks but vision saw its potential. She then capitalized on its cracks and planted flowers, which the pot watered without knowing. Let this resonate in your spirit: *despite your flaws, God has used you without you knowing it.* God does not need your permission to use you to be a blessing. There are times when you will not have a say in the matter. God decides and that's it. If you were told of every plan the Lord had and was doing, you would abort some.

There was an unannounced problem for the old lady when carrying the water pots on her shoulders in their different states. It was a problem of balance. As the cracked pot leaked its contents, the weight on her shoulder shifted more and more into imbalance, but her focus was not on the discomfort. The internal joy of seeing the flowers bloom eradicated the pain of imbalance. You need to be cognizant enough to appreciate others' cracks and flaws which will require empathy and might cause you pain. However, it's worth it.

This is similar to what happened with the Apostle Peter. Peter was the cursing and fighting disciple. He denied Jesus and fled the scene. However, after Jesus' resurrection, He said, "call my disciples and Peter." In other words, Peter, with all your flaws, come. Later, Peter preached the first message after Pentecost and in Acts 2:41 the results were tremendous. "Those who embraced his message were baptized, and about three thousand were added to the believers that day." Jesus saw beyond sight. He looked ahead in time and refused to leave this mighty preacher behind. He had cracks but was a mighty preacher.

THE DECORATED SIDE OF THE ROAD

This side of road knew that its beauty was not a result of an accident but from calculated purpose. The roadside was the recipient of a team effort between the old lady and the broken water pot. Decorating the roadside required commitment and consistency. As you renew your mind, be conscious that your desired life changes will require commitment, consistency and intentional processes.

THE HOUSE

It rejoiced weekly as freshly cut flowers were brought in and used to decorate it. The house was now friendlier, more receptive and warmer. The house did not thank the water pot. It thanked the old lady. The house spoke from its place of knowledge. It saw the old lady bringing in the flowers but failed to see the leaking water pot. By the time the cracked pot arrived home, it had stopped leaking. Like the house, you have arrived at decisions and world-views based on accessible knowledge.

However, available knowledge might not be complete truth. Don't be bound to the fear of newly learned information, even if it means our dogmas being challenged. Reject the pull to be short-sighted. You thank the old lady for the flowers. You did not see the person who conceptualized planting (in this case the old lady), the soil who gladly received the seed and fed and nurtured the seeds until they became plants. You did not see the water pot that leaked the water which was needed for the flowers to thrive. In the pursuit of renewing your minds, remember there is often more to a situation than what the eyes see.

THE NEIGHBOURS

They were happy and they looked forward to receiving. Like the house, they only saw the goodness of the old lady. You must purpose not to be angry or harbour the feeling of resentment because persons fail to appreciate the work you have done. It might be that they don't know about your contribution. Therefore, renew your mind by serving not for praises but for the joy of contributing to the enrichment of a person, community or nation.

THE FLAWED/CRACKED WATERPOT

This pot had had enough! It was too much to contain. For two years, it watched its counterpart, Mr.

Perfect deliver on its expectations. This was a source of frustration and shame for the broken pot. He was affected by comparison. What it did not know was that its own expectations were different from that of its owner. It was actually delivering what its owner expected.

The truth is: many persons are suffering from depression because they have unrealistic expectations of themselves. The broken pot did not realize its flaw was being maximized by the old lady. As you renew your mind, refrain from being consumed with what appears to be your shortcomings. Seek ways of converting those differences and see them as factors which will make you stand out. Your uniqueness is embedded in your flaws and these "flaws" may position you to be used in powerful ways. For example, Moses said, "I stutter, I cannot speak fluently," Jeremiah said, "I'm a youth." Gideon said, "My family is the least and I am the least of my family." All three highlighted their weaknesses according to societal standards, but God used them mightily.

For two years, the cracked pot's perception of self stemmed from looking through the lenses of its inabilities and imperfections. This led the pot to being ashamed and engulfed with low self-esteem. This broken pot was at a crossroad that many persons failed to cross: to accept new found truth or remain stuck in the mind of self-defeat. As we pursue mind renewal, we must become synchronized with truth, the truth that flaws, cracks and leaks, position us to do great exploits. Renew your mind with this truth; your cracks are not errors but rather the platform from which your extraordinary projects and influence can impact generations and nations.

There is no glory in being stuck at the place of self-defeat. Your reality is different from your experience or experiences. It is who or what God says about you. You have built fortified cities where poor thinking has given us the property. But like the broken pot, you must now embrace who you are and whose you are as your minds are renewed daily. You are who your mind allows you to be. The cracked pot had to embrace its transformation. It was transformed but still cracked. Too often we allow our cracks to block our transform-ation and transportation. As your mind is renewed, you now find value not in being perfect, but in pur-pose. The pot's brokenness opened or unravelled its concealed purpose. There are hidden treasures within you and your cracks serve as master of unveiling. Let's thank God for our cracks.

MIND RENEWAL KEYS

In this chapter on "Cracked Transformers" we have shared some Mind Renewal keys to help you to become a better person. Here is a summary of these keys that you can apply to your life daily or as the circumstances arise. Read and meditate on them. Pray and declare them over your life to walk in the victory God has prepared for you.

1. Your brokenness might just be your launching pad into unimaginable service.
2. Despite your flaws, God has used you without you knowing it.
3. Be conscious that your desired life changes will require commitment, consistency and intentional processes.
4. Don't be bound to the fear of newly learned information, even if it means your dogmas being challenged.
5. In the pursuit of renewing your mind, remember there is often more to a situation than what the eyes see.
6. Serve not for praises but for the joy of contributing to the enrichment of a person, community or nation.
7. Refrain from being consumed with what appears to be your shortcomings.
8. You must become synchronized with the truth that flaws cracks and leaks, position you to do great exploits.
9. You are who your mind allows you to be.
10. There is value in your imperfection.

CHAPTER 8:

VICTORY BEYOND THE BARRIERS

"Success is to be measured not so much by the position that one has reached in life as by the obstacles which he has overcome." —Booker T. Washington

CALEB'S BARRIER

As we pursue Mind Renewal, let's hear from Caleb. Moses sent twelve spies to search out the land of Canaan and they returned safely with their reports.

And they told him, and said, We came unto the land whither thou sentest us, and surely it floweth with milk and honey; and this is the fruit of it. Nevertheless the people be strong that dwell in the land, and the cities are walled, and very great: and moreover we saw the children of Anak there (Numbers 13:27-28).

The Promised Land was awesome, filled with wealth and challenges. In the English language, the conjunction "and" is used to continue a sentiment while "but" is used to signify a change in direction. So why insert "and" between wealth and challenges? For the most part, we see challenges as a negative and something we can do without. However, challenges are the backbone on which lies greatness. Every challenge has embedded in it, a breaker and a maker, failure and success. The recipient of the challenge is who decides the direction of fate. Without obstacles, you will never discover your true potential and strength. Every good thing comes with challenges. Challenges help to give balance to our lives.

And Caleb stilled the people before Moses, and said, Let us go up at once, and possess it; for we are well able to overcome it. But the men that went up with him said, We be not able to go up against the people; for they are stronger than we. And they brought up an evil report of the land which they had searched unto the children of Israel, saying, The land, through which we have gone to search it, is a land that eateth up the inhabitants thereof; and all the people that we saw in it are men of a great stature. And there we saw the giants, the sons of Anak, which come of the giants: and we were in our own sight as grasshoppers, and so we were in their sight (Numbers 13:30-33).

We see two different reports which were based on different perspectives. Caleb said, "Yes we can, let's go up now and conquer." But the other ten spies said we are not able to go up against them. The ten said, "...and we seemed to ourselves like grasshoppers." They were defeated based on their perspective. They saw giants and they were like grasshoppers. *We are how we view ourselves.* You will never be victorious from the balcony of defeat. They compared themselves to their enemies upon the rubric of the physical realm. Their perspective rendered them powerless against the challenge that stood before them. They saw not a battle but suicide. After delivering their perspective, it affected the entire camp. This highlights the need to be responsible with your perspectives. The people responded:

And wherefore hath the Lord brought us unto this land, to fall by the sword, that our wives and our children should be a prey? Were it not better for us to return into Egypt? And they said one to another, Let us make a captain, and let us return into Egypt (Numbers 14:3-4).

The thought of dying at the hands of these giants, now crushed the spirit of the congregation and they weighed the future based on the perspective of the ten. Go forward and die, go backward and live as slaves. This is a challenging place. They were prepared to discredit all the miracles of Jehovah because they perceived themselves like grasshoppers to what was before them. What about the history of the Red Sea standing before them and the enemy behind them? Didn't God deliver? Renew your mind with this indelible truth; the victories of the past are given to us to be used in the future as a reminder and encourager, that *victory lies just beyond the barriers.*

Refusing to go forward will keep you saturated in the field of barely enough, while the vastness of more than enough watches from a not so far distance. Fear paralyzes our minds and prevents us from seeing beyond it. As we renew our minds, we must begin to doubt our doubts. They were on the brink of prosperity. They saw and heard how wealthy the land was, but their minds caved to the evil of the past, where they were not free. A poor perspective has the potential to blind us to the atrocities we escaped in the past and cause us to see it now as a viable option. It's like a lady choosing to return to an abusive relationship instead of remaining alone.

What made Caleb's perspective so different? Caleb believed in God completely. God said He was taking them to give them an inheritance, a land flowing with milk and honey. As Caleb went and spied out the land, he saw the milk and honey flow. This was enough for him. He saw part B of the promise, and he was fully persuaded that part A, would be delivered by God. The same God who delivered them from the Egyptians was more than able to fulfil His promise. Caleb believed. Our belief system serves as a door, exit or entrance. In renewing your mind, never forget, strange is the man who goes against his belief system. Caleb's perspective hinged on his trust in the testimony and faithfulness of Jehovah. He had not seen or heard that God had ever failed. It is foolish to doubt that which has never failed.

SAME DOOR

Frequently, we hear the sentiments echoed of, "thanking God for open doors." However, we rarely hear persons thanking God for closed doors. The same God that opens one door closes another. A not so close scrutiny of a door will reveal that it serves two purposes—it opens and it closes. The same door that leads to the exit also leads to an entrance. The decision of direction is not the responsibility of the door but the person caught between decisions. A door can have poison on one side and the antidote on the other. The choice of residence determines life or death.

The children of Israel on their historic exodus from Egypt were confronted with a wall of water. The miraculous power of God opened a dry land door and passage for them to cross over to the other side. This was awesome! Their enemies, the Egyptians, saw this and entered the same door in pursuit of their prize. However, the door closed on them and they all perished. As we renew our minds, let us be cognizant of this truth, what is a door to someone might not be the same for you. The story below illustrates the point.

And Moses stretched out his hand over the sea; and the Lord caused the sea to go back by a strong east wind all that night, and made the sea dry land, and the waters were divided. And the children of Israel went into the midst of the sea upon the dry ground: and the waters were a wall unto them on their right hand, and on their left. And the Egyptians pursued, and went in after them to the midst of the sea, even all Pharaoh's horses, his chariots, and his horsemen. And it came to pass, that in the morning watch the Lord looked unto the host of the Egyptians through the pillar of fire and of the cloud, and troubled the host of the Egyptians.

And took off their chariot wheels, that they drove them heavily: so that the Egyptians said, Let us flee from the face of Israel; for the Lord fighteth for them against the Egyptians. And the Lord said unto Moses, Stretch out thine hand over the sea, that the waters may come again upon the Egyptians, upon their chariots, and upon their horsemen. And Moses stretched forth his hand over the sea, and the sea returned to his strength when the morning appeared; and the Egyptians fled against it; and the Lord overthrew the Egyptians in the midst of the sea. And the waters returned, and covered the chariots, and the horsemen, and all the host of Pharaoh that came into the sea after them; there remained not so much as one of them (Exodus 14: 21-28).

For the Israelites, the door through the Red Sea was a highway of deliverance, but to the Egyptians, it was a highway of death. Let's look at the Red Sea and the many purposes it served.

1. *Red Sea Barrier:* The Red Sea served as a barrier between the Israelites and their destiny. This means that anything worth having is worth fighting for. God gave the Israelites a promise and now, a major obstacle stood before them. Barriers don't always equate to a different direction. A barrier is positioned to increase the testimony of the breakthrough already orchestrated. Barriers promote creativity and determination. As you renew your mind, be conscious, humongous barriers stand

between major victories. Therefore, rather than getting flustered, get excited when you see a barrier.

We get excited because of the greatness that awaits us behind the barriers. According to Booker T. Washington, "Success is to be measured not so much by the position that one has reached in life as by the obstacles which he has overcome." Romans 8:28 states, "all things work together for good to them who love the Lord, and are called by his purpose." All things include barriers. What is that barrier that is standing between you and your purpose or destiny? If this is truly your destiny, let nothing or no one block you. Rest assured there is a way to overcome this barrier! The Israelites witnessed the instantaneous conversion of their barrier to an entrance.

2. *Red Sea Entrance:* The Israelites were faced with a dilemma that needed divine intervention and God showed up. He parted the Red Sea for His children to cross over in safety. This was their highway. God created a dry highway in the belly of the sea. This is evidence that God is not thrown into a panic mode because we have surrendered to fear and worry. You see the obstacles and the blockages but God sees an opportunity to be magnified. As we renew our minds daily, we must approach blockages with a different frame of mind. This is not to kill us, but to reveal God in a different way. This is actually a great opportunity for our knowledge of God to expand. But not just of knowledge of God, but of possibilities. You must cease limiting yourself.

3. *Red Sea Weapon of Mass Destruction:* As the Egyptians pursued with all vigour the recapture of the Israelites, they entered the same door and realized that the same door now acted against them: killing them all. They entered a door that was not opened for them. You must check who it is that has opened the doors that you have or are going through. Do we have legal or spiritual clearance for the doors we are going through? As you can see the Egyptians had neither and it ruined them.

   Are you spiritually legal where you are? When we look at the word legal, it speaks about one's constitutional rights. We have the rights of a child, rights of a wife etc. For example, same-sex marriage is legal in some countries but in the court of God, this is illegal. Common-law marriage is acceptable in the court of law but not in the court of God. Has God sanctioned your place, position, relationship, marriage etc.? A person can be physically married to one person but spiritually is married or having intercourse with several wives or husbands. There are persons who have sex partners whom they have never met in the physical realm but occasionally join them in their dreams. Additionally, some are having intercourse with past lovers.

4. *Red Sea Closed Door:* The same Red Sea that served as an entrance to the Israelites also served as a closed door to them. It blocked them from going back that way to Egypt. Egypt represented the place of bondage and ruthless working conditions. Their life was made bitter with hard service. God closed

the door as a blessing to them. The same opened door now functioned as a closed door.

A truth that we must embrace is: *seasonal openings*. Some doors come with unseen expiry dates. We tend to expect an open door to remain open forever especially if the open door was very good for us. However, like persons, some doors come for specific seasons and times. We must love the door enough to release it and move on to the next opening. Refusing to accept a closure can mean denying yourself a fresh opening. Let's look at the following account from Jessica Mehta which validates this point.

I worked for non-profits and NGOs as a grant writer, events coordinator, admin, etc. For a few years I was indifferent, but in my last two years I really burned out. In my final position, I was actually hired on as a Director and wasn't told that my job was *really* to finish up the year's project before the department was shut down. I then started working on writing and me-htafor.com, a writing services company which serves a variety of clients including Fortune 500 enterprises and major media outlets. I was making six figures within 18 months; however, I attribute that to luck, dogged ambition, and moving overseas where the cost of living was much lower and I had foreign earned income exemption.[1]

Until life's journey has come to an abrupt closure, there will forever be doors providing openings and

---

[1]   https://blog.invoiceberry.com/2016/11/25-successful-entrepreneurs-quit-jobs-passions/"

closings. The closed door you're seeing today might just be that push you now need to uncover what has been waiting for you for years. Many persons have been living below their full potential because they failed to recognize the God-given opportunity that the closed door presented. We can be so stuck in the bitterness of the closed door that we are blind to the great prospect staring us right in our faces. The victory that awaits you beyond the barriers are too much to not pursue. Therefore this is why your mind must be renewed.

MIND RENEWAL KEYS

In this chapter on "Victory Beyond the Barriers" we have shared some Mind Renewal keys to help you to become a better person. Here is a summary of these keys that you can apply to your life daily or as the circumstances arise. Read and meditate on them. Pray and declare them over your life to walk in the victory God has prepared for you.

1. The victories of the past are given to us to be used in the future as a reminder and encour-

agement, that victory lies just beyond the barriers.

2. You will never be victorious from the balcony of defeat. We must begin to doubt our doubts.

3. A poor perspective has the potential to blind us to the atrocities we escaped in the past and cause us to see it now as a viable option.

4. Our belief system serves as a door, exit or entrance.

5. Never forget, strange is the man who goes against his belief system.

6. The same door that leads to the exit also leads to an entrance. The decision of direction is not the responsibility of the door, but the person caught between decisions.

7. Anything worth having is worth fighting for.

8. A barrier is positioned to increase the testimony of the breakthrough already orchestrated.

9. Be conscious that humongous barriers stand between major victories. Instead of getting flustered, get excited when you see a barrier.

10. We must approach blockages with a different frame of mind. This is not to kill us, but to reveal God in a different way.

11. There are seasonal openings. Some doors come with unseen expiry dates.

12. The closed door you see today might just be that push you now need to uncover what has been waiting for you for years.

CHAPTER 9:

THE SUCCESS LADDER

"The ladder of success is best climbed by stepping on the rungs of opportunity." —Ayn Rand

The same ladder that takes you up, takes you down. Be clear on the location of your destiny. As we renew our minds, be willing to not be driven by the movement of the crowd but by the direction of your destiny. Neither the crowd nor the news is your compass. In pursuing your destiny and fulfilling your mandate, be purpose-driven. To accomplish this, you might need to go against the tide or the current. This requires strength, self-confidence and focus. The popular current takes us to the average, the norm, what is expected, the easy. But what if your destiny is waiting for you in the abyss of the uncommon or unpopular? Let's look at Isaac's famine experience in Genesis 26:1-14:

And there was a famine in the land, beside the first famine that was in the days of Abraham. And Isaac went unto Abimelech king of the Philistines unto Gerar.

And the Lord appeared unto him, and said, Go not down into Egypt; dwell in the land which I shall tell thee of: Sojourn in this land, and I will be with thee, and will bless thee; for unto thee, and unto thy seed, I will give all these countries, and I will perform the oath which I sware unto Abraham thy father; And I will make thy seed to multiply as the stars of heaven, and will give unto thy seed all these countries; and in thy seed shall all the nations of the earth be blessed; Because that Abraham obeyed my voice, and kept my charge, my commandments, my statutes, and my laws. And Isaac dwelt in Gerar:

And the men of the place asked him of his wife; and he said, She is my sister: for he feared to say, She is my wife; lest, said he, the men of the place should kill me for Rebekah; because she was fair to look upon.

And it came to pass, when he had been there a long time, that Abimelech king of the Philistines looked out at a window, and saw, and, behold, Isaac was sporting with Rebekah his wife. And Abimelech called Isaac, and said, Behold, of a surety she is thy wife; and how saidst thou, She is my sister? And Isaac said unto him, Because I said, Lest I die for her. And Abimelech said, What is this thou hast done unto us? one of the people might lightly have lien with thy wife, and thou shouldest have brought guiltiness upon us. And Abimelech charged all his people, saying, He that toucheth this man or his wife shall surely be put to death. Then Isaac sowed in that land, and received in the same year an hundredfold: and the Lord blessed him. And the man waxed great, and went forward, and grew until he became very great: For he had possession of flocks, and possession of herds, and great store of servants: and the Philistines envied him (Genesis 26:1-14).

Isaac went against the tide. He sowed in the time of famine and received an increase of a hundredfold. That is a worthwhile investment. Your increase might just be in the direction which only the brave dare to tread. His heroic victory was not found in floating downstream but in swimming upstream against the tide. To experience similar results means more work, effort, dedication, commitment and obedience to God.

Isaac was envied and not for his resilience or long working hours but for his success. Envy is wasted energy and time. That energy could have been utilized to copy the efforts of the envied one. If you're going to envy someone, don't start at their success but at their pain. Never forget this, until you are prepared to desire the suffering that precedes the glory, then be silent. You want the glory but not the story.

According to Barack Obama, "Change will not come if we wait for some other person or some other time. We are the ones we've been waiting for. We are the change that we seek."

As we renew our minds, let us stop expecting everyone to celebrate our success. Remove yourself from waiting for others to show appreciation. Instead, spread your own red carpet. You laboured and committed to going against the flow of the mediocre and employed the spirit of excellence. Celebrate your achievements. Celebrate you. We celebrate independence, emancipation, birthdays, anniversaries and that's all good. But when is celebrate me day? This should be as often as possible. Everyday won't harm you. Be the first to congratulate yourself on a goal accomplished. I'm not promoting pride or thinking too much of one's self but you should not undervalue your successes either. This kind of celebration of self/accomplishments makes it easier to rejoice with others.

Isaac was resented because of his success. Success will attract new friends and see the expulsions of old friends. Pay attention to who celebrates your small victories. Stop being disappointed. The persons who celebrated your small victories may hate your massive success. As you renew your minds, note that, those who leave might not be bad persons. They are just not equipped to handle you succeeding at this level.

Within any given dimension, there can be several levels. Levels are divisions of a dimension which is the complete mass, space or area. Your success transports you from levels to levels and then dimensions. Persons who are at levels cannot comprehend dimensions. It is not enough to have crossed over from levels to dimensions, but maintenance and further growth must be advanced. The grade of thinking that saw you succeeding at levels, will not suffice at dimensions. Your thought processes must match your place of increase. The greater your success, the more is expected of you and from you. If your output remains the same, you are failing at this new place. Success comes with blessings and weight. If the weight of success outweighs the joy of success, you are no longer successful but now failing.

Stop waiting on the moment to seize you, seize the moment. As Russian Philosopher Ayn Rand states, "The ladder of success is best climbed by stepping on the rungs of opportunity." Refuse to wait for a handout opportunity. Instead pursue with all diligence, the creation of your own opportunities.

In the year 2000, I worked at a well-established hardware store as a data entry clerk. The salary was average and I had difficulty making ends meet. One day I walked the streets of *Downtown* Kingston and saw items half the prices as the ones *Uptown*. I bought one Grey Flannel cologne and resold it for the uptown price. I took the profit and bought two colognes. When I sold them I began my entrepreneurship journey. I was terminated at the hardware store because I was not giving maximum output. This created opportunity grew and grew until I started travelling overseas to purchase goods, and this I did for many years. Be willing to invest in your success. As you renew your mind, always remember, success is not the fruit of accidents, but the reward of diligent forward thinking, planning, and execution.

Be prepared to be considered mentally bankrupt as you move forward against the norm. But be encouraged. Today's mockery is tomorrow's necessity.

"Someone is sitting in the shade today because someone planted a tree a long time ago." —Warren Buffett

Like Isaac, be courageous and plant where and when no one else dares to. The regular sower plants in the scheduled time and season. While planting for the exceptional, defies logic, reasoning, and intellect. I'm willing to celebrate your achievements but I need to be empowered. If all your friends want to do is laud their success in the face of your failures, it's time to change company.

THE ILLOGICAL OPTION

Peter was not the only disciple in the boat, but he was the one who spoke. Don't let the silence of the mass remove your tongue of extraordinary desires. Outstanding achievements are not the fruits of bankrupt minds. Peter challenged Jesus, who was his superior. That which I see you doing, empower me to do it.

And in the fourth watch of the night Jesus went unto them, walking on the sea. And when the disciples saw him walking on the sea, they were troubled, saying, It is a spirit; and they cried out for fear. But straightway Jesus spake unto them, saying, Be of good cheer; it is I; be not afraid. And Peter answered him and said, Lord, if it be thou, bid me come unto thee on the water. And he said, Come. And when Peter was come down out of the ship, he walked on the water, to go to Jesus (Matthew 14:25-29).

Peter made a bold request which went against knowledge and expertise. Peter by trade was a fisherman, and understood that walking on water is not a logical option. His best bet was to remain in the boat like the others. The boat represented the place of knowledge, comfort, and safety. He made an unprecedented request, "bid me leave all that I know, my company and what makes sense." Look at the time Jesus chose to walk on the water towards his disciples. *And the boat was already a considerable distance from land, buffeted by the waves because the wind was against it."* When the wind of life is against you, rejoice! The odds against you shout: miracle is at hand, tap in. Get prepared to make some crazy requests. Renew your mind with this truth, your belief of who God is, is demonstrated by your declarations and actions. That is why, those who think they have a trivial present role or future, will always act in an insignificant manner.

Peter seized the moment of mind expansion. He was transported by faith and willingness to be different from being a boat rider to an ocean walker. Look closely, the atmosphere was rich and charged with the miraculous, but of the company of disciples, only Peter captured it. Let's renew our minds in this wise: it's easier to wait on the light at the end of the tunnel, but that's too predictable. Why not light a lamp in the tunnel? The tunnel is what we make it to be. It can be the place of loneliness, uncertainty, depression, and chaos. Or we can transform it into a place of new beginnings, the place where creativity meets opportunity, or where the supernatural is manifested in the natural realm. The ladder of success might not be easy but it is worth climbing. Let nothing or anyone prevent you from pursuing the success that awaits you.

MIND RENEWAL KEYS

In this chapter on "The Success Ladder" we have shared some Mind Renewal keys to help you to become a better person. Here is a summary of these keys that you can apply to your life daily or as the circumstances arise. Read and meditate on them. Pray and declare them over your life to walk in the victory God has prepared for you.

1. Neither the crowd nor the news is your compass, flow in the direction of your destiny.
2. If you're going to envy someone, don't start at their success but at their pain. Never forget this, until you are prepared to desire the suffering that precedes the glory, then be silent.
3. Stop expecting everyone to celebrate your success.
4. Those who leave might not be bad persons. They are just not equipped to handle you succeeding at this level.
5. Success comes with blessings and weight.
6. Success is not the fruit of accidents.

7. Don't let the silence of the mass remove your tongue of extraordinary desires.

8. It's easier to wait on the light at the end of the tunnel, but that's too predictable. Why not light a lamp in the tunnel? The tunnel is what we make it to be.

CHAPTER 10:

A BETTER ME

"Do unto others as you would have them do unto you." (Matthew 7:12, NIV).

There you are, sitting, fatigued, feeling discombobulated and like a failure. This was not in the budget. Two years into the marriage and now it's officially over! If she/he was a better person, helped with the children, paid more attention, remembered our anniversary and my birth date, if only his/her family stayed out of our affairs, and only if she/he handled our finances better, then we would still be married. In this our quest for mind renewal, let us avoid the temptation to be so busy seeing the faults of the other that we begin to see ourselves as angels. It is time for us to introspect. What was your contribution to the demise of the relationship, be it a marriage, a job or a friendship? The late pop star Michael Jackson sang it this way:

I'm starting with the man in the mirror
I'm asking him to change his ways
And no message could have been any clearer
If you wanna make the world a better place
Take a look at yourself and then make a change.

How can I be a better me? A better me, is not far-fetched but one confined in the deepest part of my being. As I pursued a better me, I was confronted with some simple yet powerful guidelines. It began one year as the New Year was approaching, and on the lips of many were New Year's resolutions. I thought about what that should be, having faltered in my many previous attempts. Then I decided on, Matthew 7:12, "Therefore all things whatsoever ye would that men should do to you, do ye even so to them: for this is the law and the prophets."

This forced me to look at the things I personally hated or those things I would not want to be done to me. My list was long. Take the time to write your list. I would not want to be cheated on, lied to, lied on, mistreated, not given my due honour and the list goes on. Now, I must do likewise to all mankind who cross my path. Since that New Year's resolution, I've not made another because I'm still working on that one. As we renew our minds, let's change the world one person at a time, starting with yourself. Reggae singer Jah Cure in his famous song, "Prison a Nuh Bed a Rose" said, "I swear I can be a better man."

A better you, will mean failing and restarting. Let us look at how the apostle Paul said it in Romans 7: 21, "I find then a law, that when I have a will to do good, evil is present with me." Paul made it abundantly clear that you are not naturally good and for the good to be seen in you, will require intent and dedication. For the better you to surpass the evil you, Mind Renewal is imperative. In challenging ourselves to become better, we will have failures and successes.

After Peter categorically declared before Jesus' crucifixion that he would never deny him. Jesus said to him, "Peter before the cock crows thrice you will deny me." Furthermore, Jesus said, "And the Lord said, Simon, Simon, behold, Satan hath desired to have you, that he may sift you as wheat: but I have prayed for thee, that thy faith fail not: and when thou art converted, strengthen thy brethren" (Luke 22:31-32). Jesus was trying to get Peter to see that although he desired to do good, evil would overtake him. The better you will give way to the weaker you. Jesus' words came to pass. Peter denied him three times. But although Peter failed, he didn't crash at the roadblock. The same Peter became a loyal follower of Christ dying a martyr's death. This is chronicled in the "Amazing Bible Timeline with World History."

Simon, called Peter by Christ, died 33-34 years after the death of Christ. According to Smith's Bible Dictionary, there is 'satisfactory evidence that he and Paul were the founders of the church at Rome and died in that city. The time and manner of the apostle's martyrdom are less certain. According to the early writers, he died at or about the same time with Paul, and in the Neronian persecution, A.D. 67, 68. All agree that he was crucified. Origen says that Peter felt himself to be unworthy to be put to death in the same manner as his Master, and was, therefore, at his request, crucified with his head downward.

Peter, after the death and resurrection of Jesus became a better person. Sometimes it takes the death of someone or something for us to discover ourselves. For some it's the death of a job, wealth, marriage or health. In the prophet Isaiah's case it was after the death of King Uzziah, when he saw the Lord high and lifted up. What is it that needs to die for you to become a better you? Is it your pride, arrogance or conceitedness? As I pursued the unravelling of the better me, I came to terms with the importance of quick forgiveness. Quick forgiveness is rejecting the opportunity of festering ills and negative feelings. Entrepreneur John Rampton cites the following as a tool to become a better you.

Practice Forgiveness: Joyce Marter, LCPC, suggests you forgive and let go of resentment. She notes, "If for no other reason than for yourself, forgive to untether yourself from the negative experiences of the past. Take time to meditate, and give thanks for the wisdom and knowledge gained from your suffering. Practice the mantra, 'I forgive you and I release you.'"

I believe in talking to myself, and I recommend you do the same. Replay yesterday's conversations. Ask yourself questions like: what can I do today that was not done yesterday? Did I handle that argument well? Was I fair in my appraisal? Before I submit this report, am I telling the whole truth? If I were not me, would I want to marry me? Similarly, if I were my child, would I want me as a father/mother? Am I a good neighbour, a good friend? We become the "better us" when we can be honest with ourselves about the positives and the negatives.

To become a better you, you will have to address issues that have been hidden in your closet of unpleasantries. These could be unresolved hurts, submission issues, envy in relationships, insecurities, love for malice, lying, being rebellious and you can add your individual truth to this list. To become a better you, stop projecting the pain of failed relationships unto the innocent. Stop using the victim card.

To become a better you, you need to take responsibilities for your actions whether good or bad. Watch this, Jamaican reggae artist, Shaggy did a song depicting irresponsibility that went straight to the top of the charts. It was popular among the youths and the general population.

Look at the words [Pre-Chorus: Rikrok and (Shaggy)]

But she caught me on the counter (wasn't me),
Saw me banging' on the sofa (wasn't me),
I even had her in the shower (wasn't me),
She even caught me on camera (wasn't me),
She saw the marks on my shoulder (wasn't me),
Heard the words that I told her (wasn't me),
Heard the scream getting louder (wasn't me),
She stayed until it was over.

Similarly, in the account of David and Bathsheba, we see the King failing to take responsibility for his sinful actions (2 Samuel 11). Like Shaggy, David was saying, "it wasn't me." He shifted responsibility and in covering up, he was led into further sin. Let's break down David's actions which reflects how irresponsibility can lead to further sin.

1. *He partook of that which was not legally his.* After David learned that Bathsheba was married, the story should have ended abruptly. However he proceeded and had intercourse with her. Her married status rendered her illegal to him. The better you abhors adultery.

2. *He refused to take responsibility for the pregnancy.* David received information that Bathsheba was pregnant and he sent for her husband from the battle field. At first glance, this seems an honorable action. A man filled with regret and needs to confess. But deception prevailed.

3. *He was intent on perverting the course of justice.* "And David said to Uriah, Go down to thy house, and wash thy feet" (2 Samuel 11:8b). This instruction was imbedded with falsification.

4. *He was hypocritical in his friendship and appreciation.* "And Uriah departed out of the king's house, and there followed him a mess of meat from the king and when David had called him, he did eat and drink before him; and he made him drunk" (2 Samuel 11:13a). David's gifts were not genuine as they came from a polluted heart. Where is your gift

coming from? We must be careful, not every well-packaged parcel is indeed intended for our good.

David not only tried to bribe Uriah with pleasantries of his wife but got him intoxicated, in an effort to have him not focus or think logically. This would lead him to go home and have sex with his wife. He tried to manipulate Uriah's thinking and decision-making process just to have his own way. You need to be careful of manipulators. They are everywhere and come in different forms. As you renew your mind to become a better you, ensure the place from which you give is genuine. Reject the offer of being named among devious manipulators.

5. *He failed to give honour where honour was due.* Uriah expressed to David, he cannot go in to have sexual relationship with his wife knowing that the Ark of Covenant and his fellow soldiers are at war. Uriah displayed loyalty and great honour. Yet David dishonored him. In renewing our minds, let us assassinate our selfish desires and give honor where it is due.

6. *He plotted the death of the innocent.* David failed at manipulating Uriah into blindfolded fatherhood. He then orchestrated the death of a soldier more loyal than himself. Uriah was killed not for an offence committed but because he was a committed and loyal soldier. David the King failed to do good.

Based on these six consequences, which was the greater sin, having sex with another man's wife or not taking responsibility for her pregnancy, or killing the man to hide his wrongdoing? To become a better you, a good place to start is to adopt the philosophy that "if you can't own it, don't do it." The tendency to cast the blame away from ourselves even when we are guilty is of great concern. In Genesis chapter three, Adam blamed Eve and God, and Eve blamed the serpent. Some blame the system, parents, country they were born to, economic strains, and everything except themselves. We can only grow from owning up to our errors. To become a better you, learn from your mistakes and move forward in grace.

For years, I struggled with procrastinating, but I never got the victory until I acknowledged my problem and began working against it. Author Wayne Dyer's teaching on blame is noteworthy if you are to become a better you.

All blame is a waste of time. No matter how much fault you find with another, and regardless of how much you blame him, it will not change you... Usually, making excuses is just something we can get away with, rather than challenging or changing ourselves. If you want to change and you want your life to work at a level you've never had before, then take responsibility for it.[2]

In taking responsibility, we have the task of self- control. We must guard the gates to our body. For David, his eye gate was unprotected. David saw and his heart deceived him. As husbands and wives, or someone in a

---

[2]   NaturalAwakeningMag.com (September 2009).

committed relationship, you will see other persons who are attractive, sexy, good-looking who look like the perfect being. However, you must be committed to your commitment. You did not go physically blind the day you said yes to your partner. Instead, you decided to take on or activate greater levels of self-control. David saw that which was not his and coveted it. As we renew our minds, not everything that is within our reach needs to be held. Touch not, taste not, and handle not that which is not yours. This will help you to become a better you.

MIND RENEWAL KEYS

In this chapter on "A Better Me" we have shared some Mind Renewal keys to help you to become a better person. Here is a summary of these keys that you can apply to your life daily or as the circumstances arise. Read and meditate on them. Pray and declare them over your life to walk in the victory God has prepared for you.

1. Avoid the temptation to be so busy seeing the faults of others that we begin to see ourselves as angels.

2. Let's change the world one person at a time, starting with yourself.
3. A better you, will mean failing and restarting.
4. We can only grow from owning up to our errors.
5. Practice quick forgiveness.
6. Not everything that is within your reach needs to be held.
7. We become the "better us" when we can be honest with ourselves about the positives and the negatives.
8. To become a better you, you will have to address issues that have been hidden in your closet of un-pleasantries.
9. Ensure the place from which you give is genuine.
10. Not every well-packaged parcel is indeed intended for your good.
11. Be committed to your commitment.

CHAPTER 11:

IT'S NOT ABOUT YOU

"There can be no greater gift than that of giving one's time and energy to help others without expecting anything in return." —Nelson Mandela

Some years ago, I read Rick Warren's book, *The Purpose Driven Life*. I have not gotten past the first sentence, "It's not about you." This is a powerful Mind Renewal concept that we should begin pursuing immediately, it's not all about you. This is evident in Exodus 8:5-6.

And the Lord spake unto Moses, Say unto Aaron, Stretch forth thine hand with thy rod over the streams, over the rivers, and over the ponds, and cause frogs to come up upon the land of Egypt. And Aaron stretched out his hand over the waters of

Egypt, and the frogs came up and covered the land of Egypt (Exodus 8:5-6).

God gave specific instructions. Moses, you are the leader, but you're not the one to stretch forth your hand. You might be the leader, but you're not the only available vessel. Don't be afraid to utilize the gifts and expertise of others. There is no "I" in team. Refrain from being that "I" when what is truly required is that team. As you work with the team, be conscious that the dynamics can change and where team was, you're now challenged with team members functioning in "I" mode. Moses, the leader, must understand that God will only use him to demonstrate the mighty works of God. There is no place for pride or being pumped up. If you're going to be a good leader, you must get over yourself and learn the art of servitude. You must be able to follow instructions carefully.

The following is also true. If you're going to walk with the leader, you must be willing to follow instructions. Trust the leader that s/he is hearing from God. Aaron, "God says, stretch your hand with your rod over rivers, streams, and ponds and cause frogs to come up." You're not the leader, but you are relevant. Who told you, you were insignificant? Where did that lie come from? Well, hear what the spirit of the Lord says, "It's a lie." You are positioned where you are because you are needed. Your abilities have ushered you into the team. You're not just making up numbers, and if the negative thoughts suggest that to you, then counteract it with, "the numbers were needed!" Like Aaron, you are grafted into the team without your knowledge. When the assignment was revealed to you, is not when it started.

Moses and Jehovah had a private conversation and God drafted for Aaron. There are some private conversations taking place and your name is being mentioned in a life-changing way. The leader, Moses, will never be completely remembered without Aaron being heard of. Your purpose is knitted to the leader's destiny. Without knowing about these communications, begin to thank God for causing you to be the topic of discussion in a positive life-changing way. We remember Philip and the Eunuch in Acts 8:26-40.

And the angel of the Lord spake unto Philip, saying, Arise, and go toward the south unto the way that goeth down from Jerusalem unto Gaza, which is desert. And he arose and went: and, behold, a man of Ethiopia, an eunuch of great authority under Candace queen of the Ethiopians, who had the charge of all her treasure, and had come to Jerusalem for to worship, Was returning, and sitting in his chariot read Esaias the prophet. Then the Spirit said unto Philip, Go near, and join thyself to this chariot. And Philip ran thither to him, and heard him read the prophet Esaias, and said, Understandest thou what thou readest? And he said, How can I, except some man should guide me? And he desired Philip that he would come up and sit with him. The place of the scripture which he read was this, He was led as a sheep to the slaughter; and like a lamb dumb before his shearer, so opened he not his mouth:

In his humiliation his judgment was taken away: and who shall declare his generation? For his life is taken from the earth. And the eunuch answered Philip, and said, I pray thee, of whom speaketh the prophet this? of himself, or of some other man? Then Philip opened his mouth, and began at the same scripture, and preached unto him Jesus. And as they went on their way, they came unto a certain water: and the eunuch said, See, here is water; what doth hinder me to be baptized? And Philip said, If thou believest with all thine heart, thou mayest. And he answered and said, I believe that Jesus Christ is the Son of God. And he commanded the chariot to stand still: and they went down both into the water, both Philip and the eunuch; and he baptized him. And when they were come up out of the water, the Spirit of the Lord caught away Philip, that the eunuch saw him no more: and he went on his way rejoicing. But Philip was found at Azotus: and passing through he preached in all the cities, till he came to Caesarea (Acts 8:26-40).

The Eunuch had a situation. He was reading without understanding. He desired knowledge but it evaded him. A great Mind Renewal principle is: "your situation is not foreign to God. He knows your crisis and He knows the solution." Unaware to him, the Lord had already spoken to Phillip, with his situation in mind. Even without you knowing, your victory is already being put in place. To you, it seems as though no breakthrough is near, but what you don't see is the orchestrating hand of the Lord, your God. Your life is in the hand of God. You will not need to chase after everything you desire. Truth is, your desire activates the heavens to begin manipulating things towards your benefit. What are your desires? The word of God says, "Blessed are they which do hunger and thirst after righteousness: for they shall be filled"(Matthew 5:6).

There are some things you search for and others God allows to locate you. Phillip received divine instruction to remove himself from where he was and get down to the desert. No matter what the name of your current desert, God will commission the victory he has for you, to find you! Don't be so angry at this financial, marital, emotional desert you have been riding through. God is sending help right where you are. He could have intercepted the eunuch outside of the desert. The God we serve knows where we are and will enter into our situations. He did it for the three Hebrew boys who were thrown into the fire by Nebuchadnezzar in Daniel 3. God did not prevent them from being thrown into the fire, but He showed up in the fire and saved them.

God allowed Phillip to be at the right place at the right time, so he could see the Eunuch. The on-time God will not allow you to miss your train. Renew your mind with this: "God is intentional." The train that went by before you was not yours to take. God reserved you for the best that is to come. You applied for the job. The interview went great. You met all the qualification and experience requirements, but you were not called. Why? It was not your time. You are qualified but out of timing.

Recently I flew into Miami. Our flight arrived ahead of schedule and had to make three circles. The plane was not permitted to land, because it arrived early and the traffic was heavy. Timing is important. Look at timing from the book of Ruth 1:22, "So Naomi returned, and Ruth the Moabitess, her daughter in law, with her, which returned out of the country of Moab: and they came to Bethlehem in the beginning of barley harvest." Naomi and her husband and two sons left Judah because there was a famine. They relocated to Moab, where her husband died, her sons got married and they also died. She heard that the Lord had remembered Judah and she decided to return home. She journeyed and arrived in Judah not at the time of planting but at harvest time.

In the Eunuch's case God instructed Phillip to join himself to the Eunuch's company. You must come to an understanding that you cannot dictate to God where or from whom help should come. The Eunuch was not travelling alone. Yet none of his companions were able to help. Know this, God may send help from outside your circle. Stop limiting your expectations of God. He is God. I was in Trinidad at a supermarket and the Holy Spirit spoke to me. He instructed me to pay for the groceries the person before me was cashing. I did not know the person, but God knew not just the person, but also their situation.

As you renew your mind knowing it's not about you, you should not believe you will always be on the receiving end. God used me, a stranger, to bless that shopper. Stop being upset because the person you helped has not reciprocated. That person was your assignment. You might just be their cheerleader. Know what you are to each person you meet and what they are to you.

YOUR ASSIGNMENT

Phillip knew what the Eunuch did not know. The eunuch was his assignment. You can work your assignment without broadcasting it. Stay close to your assignment. The Eunuch invited Phillip to sit with him. When opportunity knocks, kick off the door. Capture the extended hand. There is no need to bribe, lie or fight against someone who is already in close proximity. Know this, if God gave you the assignment, you don't have to force your way in, and the door will be opened unto you, at the right time. The God who sent you on the assignment will cause the eyes of those in authority to take notice of you.

Your assignment brings about changes. First, he was running beside him but now he is riding with him. You will never be the same having pursued an assignment. Obedience is the root of success. Notice what happened in Acts 8:36-39.

And as they went on their way, they came unto a certain water: and the eunuch said, See, here is water; what doth hinder me to be baptized? And Philip said, If thou believest with all thine heart, thou mayest. And he answered and said, I believe that Jesus Christ is the Son of God. And he commanded the chariot to stand still: and they went down both into the water, both Philip and the eunuch; and he baptized him. And when they were come up out of the water, the Spirit of the Lord caught away Philip, that the eunuch saw him no more: and he went on his way rejoicing (Acts 8:36-39).

In the desert, we see water, in such quantity that baptism was possible. I don't know if the water was there before or if it remained after, but we know it was there as they approached. Don't be so consumed with the where and how of the provision, work it. Do as the old proverb says: "drink the milk and don't count the cow." It is imperative to know when an assignment is complete. As we renew our minds, let us purpose to never overwork an assignment.

SELFLESS ACTS

In the book of Ruth, we see Naomi upon her return to her native land, saying to her greeters, "don't call me Naomi, call me Mara, for the Lord, has dealt with me bitterly." Naomi spoke from the place of grief having lost her husband, two sons, and one daughter- in-law. She was stripped of that which was precious to her. All that she had left was Ruth, her youngest daughter-in- law. In Ruth chapter 3 verse 1, we see the stripped Naomi saying to Ruth her daughter-in-law, "My daughter, shall I not seek rest for thee that it may be well with thee?" In renewing our minds, we must get to the place where the wrongs done to us or the negative situations or circumstances do not prevent us or block us from being a blessing to someone. In so doing, we come to a place of maturity so that in spite of our own failures, we seek the betterment of others.

The encouragement of acting selflessly is echoed in Philippians 2:3 "let nothing be done through strife or vainglory, but in lowliness of mind let each esteem the

other better than themselves." We are living in a society which tells us as the Jamaican proverb says: "thy
man look out for thyself," in other words, it's me, myself, and I. We need to change this as we renew our
minds. Romans 12:10 tells us that we are to be kindly
affectionate one to another in brotherly love; in honour preferring one another. At times, we are so selfish
that it would pain us to think of others except for family members and associates. But someone once said,
"selflessness does not end at loving our family and
friends."

Scripture tells us to extend this even to our enemies.
Jesus volunteered by giving His life that we may live and
have fellowship with Him, that was the most selfless act.
"No one can take my life from me. I sacrifice it voluntar-
ily" (John 10:18, NLT). He's asking us to do the same by
giving our time and resources to help others. In my es-
timation, one of my greatest satisfaction and joy in doing
a kind act is to see a need met, and to see a smile on a
face when a gentle touch is given and a kind word
spoken. That I believe brings joy to my Father's heart because what we do for others we do unto Him.

DAVID'S SELFLESS ACT

As you peruse the book of 1 Samuel commencing at
chapter 13, you see King Saul's eldest son Jonathan. He
became very close to David a servant of his father. King
Saul desired to kill David but Jonathan saved his friend
and helped him to escape. Jonathan knew that some-
day David would inherit the throne that he should

have inherited himself, but his soul was knit to David in such a way that it didn't matter. Jonathan did not know that, after his death, his son Mephibosheth would be a permanent guest at King David's table. Mephibosheth was crippled after he was dropped by his nurse when she tried to save his life. Please renew your mind with this truth, not every bad result originated from an evil intent. Take the needed time to review the intent. David was kind to Mephibosheth only because Jonathan did a selfless act. He sacrificed his inheritance in sparing David's life from the hands of his God-rejected father, Saul.

You have not really lived until you have done something for someone who can never repay you. So let us live. You *don't* need reasons to help God's people. Do it and expect nothing in return. When you give to others you are actually lending to God (Proverbs 19:17). One selfless act can change the course of generations. One act of kindness can cause the enemy's plan against you to malfunction. One selfless act can move God's hand on your behalf and position you for greatness (and greatness here means fulfilling your God-given mandates/ assignments).

MOTIVES

To become a better you, closely examine your motives. A certain man got baptized and he started crying in the water. Many persons believed it was the spirit of God moving upon him. However, what they did not know was his motive or reason for crying. He had been having an affair with a lady on the choir. When he looked at her knowing it was good but it is now over, he cried. She started crying and the church thought she was just happy for him. What is your motive?

A simple meaning of "motive" is the reason for doing something. Knowingly and unknowingly we do have motives as individuals and don't even realize it. Why we do the things we do? We must understand that everything we do, is propelled by a primary and a secondary motive and even a tertiary one. Why do you attend the church that you go to? You commit yourself to be present at most meetings, be it Sunday, Saturday, mid-week etc. What are your motives? As we renew our minds and progress to being better persons, we cannot avoid looking at our motives.

There are genuine and non-genuine motives. Non-genuine motives are wrapped in selfishness. Genuine motives are found outside the parameters of self. When your motives are not self-pleasing, you carry a glow, a recognition that cannot be hidden. Selfishness is what hides you from your Destiny helpers and your purpose.

In the book of Ruth, we see genuine motive at its best. Ruth went to glean in an attempt to provide for herself and her mother-in-law. Ruth's motive was to provide for her mother-in-law. She refused to let the elderly lady go out to work. Her motive caused her to do that which was reserved for the poor-gleaning. This is the act of reaping the remaining crops from fields after they have been harvested by planters.

Genuine motives will drive you to put others before you. Boaz ordered that Ruth be allowed not only at the edges but into the whole field. Boaz, in other words, said "you are not at the place that you have earned."

The system dictates that you be at the edge, however, you have earned a place in the prime lot because of your good motives. Your good motives will produce major shifts in your life.

When we pray for things with wrong motives our prayers go unanswered. Be true and real with God. He already knows what we think of before we even ask. This is what He requires. Many of the tears and pity party that we embellish are not necessary. What we need is the "shield of faith." To lift high and ward off the darts of doubt and fear which lead to us mingling in wrong motives. In Ephesians 6, the writer speaks of the shield of faith as being part of the whole armour of God. The armor of God is the Word of God.

You can have the right motive and still commit a sin or do wrong. The right motive in disobedience is no excuse. In John 6:26 "Jesus answered them and said, Verily, verily, I say unto you, Ye seek me, not because ye saw the miracles, but because ye did eat of the loaves, and were filled."

Here, Jesus addressed the matter of motive. Jesus was not fooled by the crowd seeking after Him. He saw right through them. He saw their motive. This came after Jesus multiplied the fish and the bread and fed 5000 men plus women and children. What a great miracle, a notable one! Jesus said, that's not the reason you are seeking my company. It is because you were filled. They were not seeking Jesus himself. Jesus taught us a powerful lesson: don't be driven by the crowd.

May God help us to have the right motives in all that we do and say. The enemy will want us to think otherwise but we will have to tell him that he's the father of lies. Primary motive speaks to the main and true reason behind our actions. In the case mentioned in St. John 6, their primary motive was their belly. A spiritual daughter of mine, Stacey Garvey shared the following:

I was deep in thought once when I shared a vision of me preaching to someone, and all I could talk about was what I was wearing and how good I looked. My friend then asked if that was the reason I was excited about the vision or was it because I was being used by God. That thing caused deep reflection so much that I went into a time of repentance for my motives towards the Gospel of Jesus Christ. I was wrong. I just wanted the glory and not God.

There was a period of time in my life where I used to seek God just to help me with my problems. I would only fast when I had issues. Then one day I heard a song "I surrender all to you, withholding nothing. "My spirit began weeping until my physical body wept before God. All this time being a Christian I had no love for Jesus. I went before God and I prayed and he taught me love. God allowed me to love him in such a way that my problems became inferior. I loved God so much that I became willing to suffer for him. I learned that long-suffering was a gift and I embraced it.

Now when I fast it's for a relationship with God. He already said in His word He will supply all our needs. So now my motive for going to church, ministering and serving God is just love. Now, I want to share the good news of how I found Him and fell in love with Him so others will love and want to be with Him too.

As you pursue Mind Renewal with the awareness, "It's not about you." Please examine what is your motive. Is God pleased with your motive or do you need to adjust? Are you being selfish?

MIND RENEWAL KEYS

In this chapter on "It's Not About You" we have shared some Mind Renewal keys to help you to become a better person. Here is a summary of these keys that you can apply to your life daily or as the circumstances arise. Read and meditate on them. Pray and declare them over your life to walk in the victory God has prepared for you.

1. It's not all about you.
2. Good leaders are first servants.
3. Your situation is not foreign to God. He knows your crisis and He knows the solution.
4. You cannot dictate to God where or from whom your help should come.
5. Know this, if God gave you the assignment, you don't have to force your way in, and the door will be opened unto you, at the right time.

6. Don't be so consumed with the where and how of the provision, work it.
7. It is imperative to know when an assignment is finished. Purpose to never overwork an assignment.
8. You must get to the place where the wrongs done to you or the negative situations or circumstances do not prevent you from being a blessing to someone.
9. You have not really lived until you have done something for someone who can never repay you. So let us live.
10. Selfishness is what hides you from your Destiny helpers and your purpose.

CHAPTER 12:

WHAT IS YOUR REALITY?

"Refrain from concluding failure where you have not explored." —Leostone Morrison

The BIG question is: what is your reality? According to the English Oxford Living Dictionary, "reality is the state of things as they actually exist, as opposed to an idealistic or notional idea of them." Based on the definition, our reality is what is actually in present existence. As you renew your mind, a firm differentiation must be made between temporary and permanent realities. One's present or ongoing situation and circumstances should not be confused with being their only reality. Situations are temporary reality and should not overshadow permanent realities.

SUICIDE

Suicide is the act of killing oneself or ending one's own life. It is a decision of finality. There are seven recorded cases in the Bible of suicide but we will cite two.

1. Judas (Mathew 27: 3-5): Then Judas, which had betrayed him, when he saw that he was condemned, repented himself, and brought again the thirty pieces of silver to the chief priests and elders, saying, I have sinned in that I have betrayed the innocent blood. And they said, what is that to us? See thou to that. And he cast down the pieces of silver in the temple, and departed, and went and hanged himself.

2. Samson (Judges 16:30): And Samson said, Let me die with the Philistines. And he bowed himself with all his might; and the house fell upon the lords, and upon all the people that were therein. So the dead which he slew at his death were more than they which he slew in his life.

Suicide as seen from the biblical examples is not a new phenomenon. It does not discriminate. Regardless of race, age, location or position, suicide is the choice of some. Judas was a disciple of Jesus and Samson was a Judge of Israel, yet both committed suicide. Unlike many suicide victims, 13-year-old Davion Johnson, a former student at the Belmont High School in Jamaica, made a video and posted it on social media.

The following is the verbatim record of his final words.

Welcome! This is my first video *that I made about why I killed myself.*

You probably know by now that I am dead, or maybe I was saved and am in the hospital. Regardless of which, *I am not sure but I never want to be saved again.*

The first time I tried suicide, I never wanted to be saved. I allowed myself to be saved because I couldn't stand the pain.

#1 reason why I killed myself is that I take insults very seriously. For example when someone says I act like an idiot, like what my aunt Joy would always say, I take her statement seriously and it makes me feel very bad. Every time I try to be nice it just doesn't work.

I never like when people swear at me especially my aunt Joy who almost every day would complain about me.

#2 reason why I killed myself is because my school work is very hard and I know for sure I won't pass my exams. I know if I don't pass I won't be able to go to school so it doesn't make any sense I try when I won't get a good grade.

Often times I get bullied at school. I also would fight. I have stopped the fighting now. Only one fight I have gotten into when I was at Belmont High in first grade.

I hate to be on the school bus at times as the kids always act like idiots and would always be slapping me in my head all the time.

I wish I could shoot and kill them all. That was what I wanted to do when I grow up for the way I was treated.

I said, "no, it's better I kill myself which is the better way."

You have to be careful of the words you say to your kids because they might also take it seriously and kill themselves like me.

Later... Rest in Peace....

Without trying to belittle how the late Davion felt, it is clear he was torn between a situation and reality. If we pay close attention, we see he spoke in the future tense as though it happened already. Although speaking in the future tense, he was not sure of the permanent reality (whether he was saved and in the hospital or dead). He then said, *"The first time I tried suicide, I never wanted to be saved."* This tells us, he was fixated in his reality of being dead. Although the first attempt failed, he never left the concluded reality of being dead. He was not speaking based on his temporary situation, but rather the permanent reality (he created in his mind). His reality was that, he was already dead. Davion then said, *"I allowed myself to be saved because I couldn't stand the pain."*

Please note, the pain was not a deterrent, but rather the push to make the fulfilment of his reality less painful and complete. He envisioned the end but the pain was an obstacle. Now he must evade the pain and fulfil his reality. He purposed that nothing would hinder his reality from being manifested. Everyone must see what he has seen. Davion's words have proven the adage, "sticks and stone can break my bones, but words can do me no harm," to be a fallacy. He said the #1 reason why I killed my self is that I take insults very seriously. As you renew your mind, be cognizant of this truth, you don't have control over what is said to you but how you receive and respond to it is within your power. And that is what matters. You must also be very careful of the words you speak towards each other.

An old wise saying is, "if you don't have good to say, don't say anything." He concluded that whenever he tried to be nice, it did not work. He developed a negative perception of himself. This affected his self-esteem and worth. Young Davion was bombarded from many angles, as though he was boxed in. He was adamant he would not pass his exams. In essence, he created the reality of exam failure even before attempting. Other options were available but were not explored. As you aggressively seek to navigate between coerced reality and genuine reality, refrain from concluding that which has not been explored. What are the available options that are yet to be explored?

He continued, *"I said, 'no, it's better I kill myself which is the better way."* He made a concerted decision after processing his realities. And he arrived where he began—death. The reality he determined for himself was: "It's better off being dead." Before he ended his recording by saying, "Rest in Peace" he warned everyone to be careful of the words we use to others. Treat others how you would want to be treated. Davion saw himself dead and spoke of himself as being dead.

His temporary situation is where he was being bullied, called names, cursed and complained on almost every day. Davion acted upon his determined reality and committed suicide. He was shut out from seeing anything beyond death. This was his decision of finality; it had to be done.

As we purpose to renew our minds, we must differentiate between coerced reality and true reality. Coerced realities are not permanent but consist of elements of overwhelming quantities and value. These are temporary but push a person to make a permanent decision. They are fueled by the situations and circumstances being lived at the present moment and are associated with feelings that are currently evident. A deep failure is being trapped in our self-created reality. The existing negatives are condemning agents, telling us there is no way out. A prisoner in one's own body is worse than a man locked behind prison bars. A trapped mind tends to internalize every situation, creating a blurry view of positive possibilities. Similarly, Davion was in such a state and operated within a vacuum that recycled every care, failure, torment and ridicule.

Now, imagine being exposed to poverty from birth, being called dirt poor and adjectives such as incompetent, sluggard and good-for-nothing are thrown at you. The words, the insults, and the reflection of poor stare back at you. Now you wrestle with either accepting your situation as final or embracing a better life outside of what you are yet to see. Many persons have found themselves 'stuck'—stuck in the impermanent seasons of life. These seasons, whilst some may last years, are exactly that—seasonal! Their minds have created walls dividing the truth of what lies beyond. On the other side is the true reality.

The true reality is what God has said about you. According to Romans 8:1, "There is therefore now no condemnation to them which are in Christ Jesus, who walk not after the flesh, but after the Spirit." There is a blueprint for every life with details of every day. The word of God says, "Thine eyes did see my substance, yet being unperfect; and in thy book all my members were written, which in continuance were fashioned, when as yet there was none of them" (Psalm 139:16). This is the reality that a crowded mind fails to accept and pursue. If every day is known and already established by God, it simply means that every single situation, whether good or bad, is a catalyst for future victories.

Here is a missed truth: *what God said about you is your present existence and your reality.* We must remember that His words cannot return unto Him void. God says you are healed and the doctors say you have three months to live. Two reports, whose will you believe? The doctor speaks from your condition, a medical perspective and God speaks from being all knowing. Unfortunately, many persons choose to live in the situational reality because they are blinded to the truth that another option is available. The general experience is a significant gap between what God says (true reality) and where persons are (situational reality). The path to the promised reality is indeed rampant with battles that are fought in the mind. Therefore, the choice to defeat the internal war rests with the will-power to walk into your God-ordained reality of your existence.

As we renew our minds, let us reject the temptation to give birth from the bed of self-determined reality, but rather lock into the vision of the reality already prepared by God. We will be the victims of confusion until our minds have deciphered the presenting realities and decide on the healthy way forward. It can be argued that what you focus on becomes the centre of what's magnified. You have the awesome responsibility of choosing which reality you're going to live with. In renewing our minds, let us embrace God's truth as our temporary and permanent reality.

MIND RENEWAL KEYS

In this chapter on "What is your Reality?" we have shared some Mind Renewal keys to help you to become a better person. Here is a summary of these keys that you can apply to your life daily or as the circumstances arise. Read and meditate on them. Pray and declare them over your life to walk in the victory God has prepared for you.

1. Situations are temporary realities and should not overshadow permanent realities.
2. A firm differentiation must be made between temporary and permanent realities. One's

present or ongoing situation and circumstances should not be confused with being their only reality.

3. Be cognizant of this truth, you don't have control over what is said to you but how you receive and respond to it is within your power.

4. As you aggressively seek to navigate between coerced reality and genuine reality, refrain from concluding that which has not been explored.

5. You must differentiate between coerced reality and true reality.

6. A trapped mind tends to internalize every situation, creating a blurry view of positive possibilities.

7. Let us reject the temptation to give birth from the bed of self-determined reality, but rather lock into the vision of the reality already prepared by God.

8. We will be the victims of confusion until our minds have deciphered the present realities and decide on the healthy way forward.

9. The choice to defeat the internal war rests with the will-power to walk into the God-ordained reality of your existence.

CHAPTER 13:

DIVINE PURPOSE

"The effect of an evil done to you, depends on you. You can choose between it being a destiny helper or a destiny destroyer." —Leostone Morrison

You cannot completely renew your mind without recognizing the need to fulfil your primary goal - your divine purpose. It's time to really think about pursuing your purpose as designated by God. What you should appreciate is that He is not asking you to do anything to which He did not subject Himself. Look at what He was subjected to in fulfilling His purpose towards mankind. Remember, He had the power to prevent all evil against Him, but He subjected Himself to abuse from His own creation. Those for whom you have laboured might just be your abusers. If that happens, you're in good company.

To fulfil His purpose to mankind, Jesus who is eternal, had to subject himself to being clothed in the mortal form of man. He was able to feel all pain, hunger and death. Jesus stepped down from His place of glory and came into a sinful world just to fulfil His purpose. What are we saying? Jesus had to give up several things in order to fulfil His purpose. Are you willing to give up what's necessary in order to fulfil your divine purpose? If your purpose costs you nothing, it's not divine. A good prayer is, *God help me to give up ANY necessity in order for your purpose to be fulfilled.*

The greatest thing to give up is your will. Jesus demonstrated this when He said to His Father "not my will but thine be done" (Luke 22:42). He demonstrated what is expected of us. When you renew your mind, it takes you to the place of erasing your own will, that will of retaliating, getting even, quitting, disobeying and having your own way. Our will is clouded by our humanity but the will of God is pure.

Stacey Garvey reminds us that, giving up your will is one of the hardest and harshest lessons to learn. She again shared the following:

I remember when God said, 'give me you!' It was challenging but then the Word taught me to trust God. And in trusting God, I gave up my will to Him. I delayed my own destiny because I refused to submit to the will of God. Sometimes when we want something really bad, we should second guess it because God always has better. The flesh will deceive us to miss what God has by looking on our desire so much that we forget to seek God about His will.

This is serious Mind Renewal. If our will is not exchanged for the will of Jesus, we shall never accomplish our purpose. Never!

After we decide to submit and pursue that submission, we must also submit to the timing of God. Now that is the hard part. We see timing being emphasized in Galatians 4:4 "But when the fullness of the time was come, God sent forth his Son, made of a woman, made under the law."

Imagine Jesus watching His creation suffer, yet subjecting Himself to wait until the time was right. Isaiah the prophet declared, "Behold, a virgin shall conceive, and bear a son, and shall call his name Immanuel" (Isaiah 7:14b). What he did not say was when and which virgin. He didn't know but God knew. Until Mary's mother and father came together and gave birth to her, and she was of mature age, Jesus had to wait. Renew your mind with this truth: there are persons waiting on you to come into alignment with your purpose. Your purpose is not in isolation. There are persons who are instrumental in helping you fulfil your mission.

Before you were conceived, your destiny helpers were already decided. For example, John the Baptist, Jesus' cousin was the forerunner to Jesus. God positioned John to announce Jesus as the Messiah. Never fail to acknowledge those who set the stage for you. Some trail was prepared for you and others you will have to blaze. Failure to submit to God's timing will lead to us getting Ishmael instead of Isaac.

God told Abraham he will get a son by his wife Sarai. He went ahead of God and got Ishmael with Hagar. God, however, kept His promise and gave the promised child, Isaac. When the timing was right according to God, not man, God sent Jesus. Jesus came not into wealth or fame but as a humble child. We miss that as we say, "I want to be more and more like Jesus." Truth is, where is our humility? We have missed it so badly that we have forgotten where we lost it. This was one of the reasons why Jesus was rejected. He did not come in earthly majesty. Yet, we His subjects, sometimes forget what humility is.

SUBMISSION TO DIVINE PURPOSE

Jonah rejected the divine assignment he received from God as recorded in the book of Jonah. This was to go to Nineveh and preach repentance. Consequently, he suffered the consequences. Unfortunately, Jonah was not the only one who suffered. The mariners lost their merchandize and experienced significant fear. Jesus submitted himself to the Holy Spirit in His pursuit of His divine purpose. According to Mathew 4:1, "Then Jesus was led by the Spirit into the wilderness to be tempted by the devil."

The writer of Hebrews helps us to understand why it was necessary for Jesus to be tempted.

Wherefore in all things it behoved him to be made like unto *his* brethren, that he might be a merciful and faithful high priest in things *pertaining* to God, to make reconciliation for the sins of the people. For in that he himself hath suffered being tempted, he is able to succour them that are tempted (Hebrews 2:17-18).

The success of your ministry and life will never reach its maximum potential until you submit to your divine purpose as expressed by the Holy Spirit. Ye that have ears to hear, let him hear. Jesus' submission is an example for us. Hear what the word of God says in James 4:7, "Submit yourselves therefore to God. Resist the devil, and he will flee from you" (James 4:7).

Submitting yourself to God goes beyond the physical domain. It extends to where we allow our spirit and mind to be subjected to the directives or leading of the Holy Spirit. When we have done this, we will be able to resist the devil. No resistance will be valid if our spirit and mind are not in agreement with the Spirit of God. We need to be the agreement bridge between Heaven and Earth, between the spiritual realm and the physical realm. When this is achieved, we will bring into manifestation in the physical realm what is already decided in the spiritual realm, which is *The Will of God.*

After doing a teaching on agreeing with heaven to see the manifestation in the physical realm, I walked into an office to see someone who was rightly disgruntled. The person refused to sign a document with the person's position affixed. This is because there was a delay in putting the position in black and white although the person was functioning in the capacity. The Lord allowed me to say, "sign it, by doing so, you are agreeing with heaven that this must be done. By not signing, you are saying you don't believe it's done already in the spirit realm and you're merely waiting for the earthly manifestation." The person signed. Soon after, the person received the position in writing. Even when it seems like it's not going to happen, you're frustrated and time is long spent, don't waver in your agreement with heaven. Stay the course. Push. Push. The will of God for your life must be done.

FULFIL YOUR PURPOSE

Purpose not to die before you've completed your purpose. Jesus modeled this for you. Look at John 19:30, "When Jesus, therefore, had received the vinegar, he said, It is finished: and he bowed his head, and gave up the ghost." This, He said while He was on the cross. He fulfilled His purpose. The redemption package was complete. Hallelujah! He had a purpose and He completed it. If we are going to speak like Jesus, we have to submit and go through. There are no shortcuts. BEWARE, there will be challenges, obstacles, haters, persecutors, liars and those who will also abandon you. Let's not forget, Jesus was abandoned by His closest friends—the ones whom He poured into and with whom He shared His life. Of His twelve disciples, one betrayed Him, one denied Him and one doubted Him. The others abandoned Him saved John who watched from a distance.

I remember being invited to speak at a church and as I sought the Lord for the message, I heard in my Spirit, "There is pain in the will of God." Renew your mind with this: there is purpose in your pain. There is the pain of disobedience and the pain of obedience. There is pain in the will of God but the greater pain stems from disobedience. Disobedience blocks your purpose. Your purpose will not be realized without your all. You will find your purpose in the will of God.

Some will say Jesus had an advantage because He knew his purpose and destiny. How many of us could handle knowing all Jesus knew that would befall Him and still pursue our purpose? As we continue to renew our minds, let's grasp this: not knowing everything is a gift. If you knew all that would befall you, you would mess your life up, kill your mission and derail your destiny. However, Jesus was serious about fulfilling His mandate. Look at the following in Matthew 16:21-23:

> From that time forth began Jesus to shew unto his disciples, how that he must go unto Jerusalem, and suffer many things of the elders and chief priests and scribes, and be killed, and be raised again the third day. Then Peter took him, and began to rebuke him, saying, Be it far from thee, Lord: this shall not be unto thee. But he turned, and said unto Peter, Get thee behind me, Satan: thou art an offense unto me: for thou savourest not the things that be of God, but those that be of men (Matthew 16:21-23).

> When Jesus had thus said, he was troubled in spirit, and testified, and said, Verily, verily, I say unto you, that one of you shall betray me. He then lying on Jesus' breast saith unto him, Lord, who is it? Jesus answered, He it is, to whom I shall give a sop when I have dipped it. And when he had dipped the sop, he gave it to Judas Iscariot, the son of Simon. And after the sop Satan entered into him. Then said Jesus unto him, That thou doest, do quickly (John 13:21, 25-27).

Jesus rejected Peter's words which went against his destiny. Don't allow the easy path to rob you of fulfilling your purpose. Stay your course and say "Oh Lord, help me to accept my destiny and not divert from the path." Jesus knew His destiny and the path that would lead Him to fulfilment. We know this according to Mark 10:45, "For even the Son of Man came not to be served but to serve, and to give his life as a ransom for many." Jesus told Judas, "Do your part (betrayal) quickly." In the name of Jesus, we command our Destiny Helpers to act quickly. Jesus' birth and death was in God's perfect timing. Let no time be wasted. Your Destiny Helpers must act now. No betrayal, no crucifixion. Your Destiny Helpers sometimes are the ones who disappoint you. Judas was indeed a Destiny Helper.

Now we understand that Judas played a significant role in helping Jesus to fulfil His purpose and destiny. Similarly, those who lied on you, betrayed you, fired you, and walked away from you, played a major role in helping you to fulfil your purpose. The effect of an evil done to you, depends on you. You can choose between it being a Destiny Helper or a Destiny Destroyer. The rape, molestation or the abuse from your ex-partner, what is it going to be, Destiny Helpers or Destroyers? As you renew your mind, remember it depends on you. The closed door you are wailing about now, and trying to reopen was divinely shut to prevent you from aborting the purpose. The Judas that manifested against you was used to steer you into the purpose orchestrated for you. We should occasionally thank God for our Judases.

HELP SOMEONE

"And as they came out, they found a man of Cyrene, Simon by name: him they compelled to bear his cross" (Matthew 27:32). A life-changing question is: "Will you help some complete their journey/destiny?" Can you be depended on to be a committed Destiny Helper? As you live, you will sadly come to realize that some persons are not willing to invest in the journey of others. They have gotten so selfish and individual-ized that they fail to see beyond themselves. Can we get back to the time when we sincerely queried, how can I assist you in completing your assignment, man-date or journey? I remember when we were studying, persons were acting selfishly with notes, books etc. One day a lecturer advised us that, we are not com-peting for one degree. All who complete will receive their just reward. Helping you does not prevent me from collecting my degree. The truth we miss is this: *helping in someone's journey serves as training ground for the completion of your own assignment.*

Jesus was battered, beaten, weakened and given His cross to bear. He struggled and Simon was given the charge to help Him. Simon helped Him in completing His assignment. Simon made the rest of the journey easier for Jesus. Who is it we have abandoned and caused to be suffering beyond what they can bear? We saw the pain, the abuse, the neglect, the weight and we turned a blind eye. We even pretended to be occupied, sick or out of town, just to escape helping. Truth is, I love you but if you can only be there for me when things are great, then I don't need you around. Where are you when I'm hurting, feel like giving up and distressed? Where are you when my husband/wife wants out of the marriage and I'm having suicidal thoughts?

It's disappointing when you go the extra mile and then when you need a helping hand, no one is there to even pray with you. Those expected are not there. In my good days, I was there for you. I carried you when you were broke, sick and depressed. I fasted for you as you sought direction and healing but now, you don't even answer your phone. Yet when I call from a different number, you answer.

It was not recorded that Simon was related to Jesus, nor was he a disciple. Your true Destiny Helpers might not be anyone you presently associate with. They might not even be known to you. They may not be family, associate or friends. Jesus was on His way to fulfilling His divine purpose and Simon assisted. Now, by virtue of him assisting, he connected with destiny and divinity. Persons may refrain from being your Destiny Helpers because they are not privy to your destiny mandate. If only they knew who you are, they would be flooding to help. But it would not be genuine. We must ensure our help is not done out of self-gain, where we help for something in return.

It cost Simon to help. Helping costs. But some persons are specialist in receiving and novices in giving. Always wanting persons to be our Destiny Helpers but never stopping to help someone. Recently, as I was going about my errands, I saw a situation and the Holy Spirit said, "Never be too busy to do good." Let us purpose to change. Not just focus on ourselves but look at someone else's needs. Yes, it is biblical. The writer of the book of Galatians puts it nicely:

> Brethren, if a man be overtaken in a fault, ye which are spiritual, restore such an one in the spirit of meekness; considering thyself, lest thou also be tempted. Bear ye one another's burden, and so fulfil the law of Christ (Galatians 6:1-2).

If your brother/sister has been overtaken, don't abandon that person. Carry the person back to safety. The farmer understands the need to help. When the banana tree is struggling under the weight of its figs, the farmer uses a crutch stick as support. Until the figs have come to maturity and reaped, the crutch stick remains with it. If you are a true Destiny Helper, and I confess to you a sin, what should really resonate in your spirit is the need to restore. In the army they don't leave their comrades behind to die. You are in the army of God, be someone's Destiny Helper. Give of yourself. Help someone to their place of fulfilment.

Someone shared the following with me.

> It was raining really bad last night. So I went to bed early. My mind started wandering. It was a struggle. I felt lonely. Then someone called and said, 'let's pray.' That praying together helped me.

Destiny Helpers certainly assist in various areas as directed by God. Sometimes in order for us to be helpers, God puts us in a similar situation so that our eyes can be opened to the need of others. You are positioned to help. Will you indeed help? It's about time love and unity be the order of the day. Let it begin with you. May God bless every Destiny Helper.

ABIDE IN YOUR PURPOSE

The decision to abide in your purpose will be aggressively attacked. Therefore you must be intentional in your pursuit of your purpose. The journey to your purpose might not always be comforting but it must be your focus. Guard your focus! We see in the account of Exodus 16:3, the following:

And the children of Israel said unto them, Would to God we had died by the hand of the LORD in the land of Egypt, when we sat by the flesh pots, and when we did eat bread to the full; for ye have brought us forth into this wilderness, to kill this whole assembly with hunger (Exodus 16:3).

From the text, we can easily deduce several points which I will list and discuss.

1. *A house filled by Satan is nothing compared to a bowl prepared by God.* The old folks said, "Little is much when God is in it." The children of Israel stopped short in comparing their present condition (hunger) to their past (had plenty of flesh until filled). We must be complete. The omission of necessary facts equates to lying. That was not the only comparison they needed to make. When they were full, they were in bondage. Now they are free.

One young lady said during her trying season, that the days of no food forced her into fasting. She decided to capitalize on the lack of resources within the physical and enhance the spiritual through fasting and prayer. That was wisdom. She became part of her miracle. We declare, "All things will work for our good," but we must go beyond the declaration. Be willing to be involved in your miracle. The young lady instead of murmuring about what she did not have, used her circumstance as a push into what she needed.

2. *Conditional Christians*: Unfortunately, many Christians fall into this category. All faith, worshipping, foot dancing, speaking in tongues are in order when life's conditions are favourable. But if the time changes, they slump into depression, doubting, trying to help God fix it when God is more than capable. In chapter 15 of Exodus, they danced, sang and played music. The condition was the mass destruction of their enemies. In Chapter 16, they cursed Moses. The condition was their hunger.

   You must be determined to be constant in your honouring of God. The New Testament exhorts us to pray without ceasing, not only in the good times but all seasons. Be like Job who upon receiving bad news after bad news, worshipped God. Please renew your mind with this, let the unfavourable conditions propel you into worship.

3. *The Great Exchange:* Daily we are invited to the table of exchange. Merchandisers want our money for their

products and services. The entertainment industry wants our time in exchange for their movies or songs. Nothing is without a price exchange. As we try to decipher which exchange is beneficial to us, let us not exchange a temporary situation with a permanent decision. One of the enemy's devices is to magnify a situation so big that it kills vision and challenge faith.

The great exchange takes place in both realms but it is more crucial in the spirit realm. The children of Israel did not physically go back to Egypt but their heart and soul returned. They exchanged freedom with temporary hunger for a belly full and bondage. Wow! What an exchange! The price of the belly full far outweighed the cost of freedom and temporary hunger, but they could not see that. It's like five minutes of sex for the destruction of a ministry that took years to build. Let's examine ourselves.

What exchange is taking place? Another great exchange is the swapping of sins. Persons have exchanged fornication for masturbation. The justification being, it's not with anyone and it keeps them from sinning against God. However, I challenge that argument to be flawed. While fornication is done in the physical realm, masturbation is sexual encounter in the spiritual domain. This is facilitated through thoughts, imagery and sounds. Masturbation goes against the very nature of God and design He perfectly created for mankind. It is self-pleasing, and promotes lusting. Jesus said in Matthew 5:28, "But I say unto you, that whosoever looketh on a woman to lust after her hath committed adultery with her already in his heart."

The children of Israel said they wished they had remained in bondage, to eat and die. The truth about the statement is that they knew nothing else but being subject to the Egyptians. They were in bondage a little over 400 years. All who spoke were born into slavery. What Moses sold to them was new and it meant change. Changes are not always readily and easily accepted. As you pursue abiding in your Divine purpose, you will encounter persons you must help, but they may not see the need to be helped or changed. This is what they know, a life of bondage and abuse. A renewed mind remains fixed on God instead of desiring short-term satisfaction. Hence it rejects the exchange of freedom in God for a temporary filling in bondage.

DIVINE INTERRUPTION

We see the lives of the children of Israel change by divine interruption, from slavery to freedom. Therefore, as we renew our minds, not every disturbance or interruption is demonic and comes with a negative outcome. Some are divine interruptions. These are the ones that God uses to reposition or realign you with your true purpose, mandate or calling. The Samaritan woman spoken of in John chapter 4, had such an encounter that changed her life and the life of many from her society. She said to Jesus, "I know the Messiah is coming." In other words, she believed without a doubt that the prophecy of the Christ coming would be fulfilled. She had great expectations. Jesus said to her, "I am the Christ." I am the fulfilment of the prophecy in Isaiah 7:14.

What Jesus did was to divinely interrupt her expectation with fulfilment. Know when you have switched seasons. The era of expectations has come to an end. A new chapter has begun and it's the chapter of fulfilment. A renewed mind transports you from expectations to fulfilment. You will not always be at expectation! Let's not miss this. "He left Judaea and departed again into Galilee. And he must needs go through Samaria" (John 4:3-4).

The interruption of your expectations with fulfilment is not an accident. It is purpose divinely orchestrated. It wasn't up for debate, grabs or petition. It was a must. Fulfilment must interrupt expectations. What you are stepping into is not "buck-up," accident or leftovers. This is yours.

As matter of fact, you can't even prevent it because it was *not* planned or purposed by you. This is God's doing. You're just the recipient. You have messed up so many good things in the past, and God allowed it, but not this chapter. This is the chapter where you make a mistake and God corrects it. Your prayer to the Lord *to make my crooked path straight* is at hand.

Pay attention. Jesus did not wait until she was in a righteous position to intercept or meet this Samaritan woman.

Renew your mind with this truth: it's a lie that you have to first be at a place of perfection for God to bless you. He met her in her state of sin and she still had good qualities. She was honest. Rest assured, you're not all evil. You have good qualities. She said, "I have no husband." This was said already, be honest with God for a change! It's not like he doesn't know, so who are we fooling? No one but ourselves! Honesty is still the best policy. You are not perfect but chosen. Messed up but still used by God.

Her plan was: get to the well, fill her water pot and return home. But when she came to the usual place, she encountered the unusual. Be prepared for God to change your usual. Things are not going to be the same as usual.

Moses had a similar encounter. He saw the bush burning, but in an unusual manifestation, as it was not consumed. It was on fire but not destroyed. Are you prepared and ready for God to change the usual to unusual in your life? This unusual for the Samaritan woman was so powerful that her main intent was cast through the door. She dropped her water pot. Someone needs to drop that water pot. Carry it no more. Greater is here. The great divine interruption promotes the great exchange. She went for usual water and met the living water: Jesus. What is that water pot that you have been carrying? When you have dropped your water pot, the enemy will find a chatty mouth, who thinks it's his/her job to remind you of that pot.

As you renew your mind, don't expect things to remain the same. Be open to changes. You cannot expect to still be the same after coming into the presence of the Almighty God. As God changes things, your present priorities will also change. You will realize things that were once super important will take a back seat. Persons whom you thought you could not do without, will become a memory. Things that presently hold you captive will cease to reign in your life.

Change your diet, change what you consume. You will need to change your restaurant. You cannot continue to go where junk is served and expect to eat healthy. Where you go and what you consume will determine your output. Start with getting rid of the negatives. Stop allowing the negatives to feed your spirit. If you have to cut, cut. Change from being fed by quitters. What do you think your output will be? They have never completed anything. They want the same for you. Surround yourself with finishers/completers to fulfil your Divine Purpose.

MIND RENEWAL KEYS

In this chapter on "Divine Purpose" we have shared some Mind Renewal keys to help you to become a better person. Here is a summary of these keys that you can apply to your life daily or as the circumstances arise. Read and meditate on them. Pray and declare them over your life to walk in the victory God has prepared for you.

1. There is purpose in your pain.
2. Grasp this: not knowing everything is a gift.

3. Don't allow the easy path to rob you of fulfilling your purpose.
4. Helping someone on their journey serves as training ground for the completion of your own assignment.
5. Your true Destiny Helpers might not be anyone you're presently associated with.
6. Guard your focus.
7. Let the unfavourable conditions propel you into worship.
8. Magnification of a negative situation serves to kill vision and challenge faith.
9. A renewed mind remains fixed on God instead of desiring short-term satisfaction. Hence it rejects the exchange of freedom in God for temporary filling in bondage.
10. Not every disturbance or interruption is demonic and comes with a negative outcome. Some are divine interruptions.
11. What you are stepping into is not "buck- up," accident or leftovers but divine interruption of expectation with fulfilment. (A renewed mind transports you from expectations to fulfilment).
12. It's a lie that you have to first be at a place of perfection for God to bless you. You are not perfect but chosen...Messed up but still used by God.
13. You cannot continue to go to where junk is served and expect to eat healthy.

CHAPTER 14:

BEAUTY OF SCARS

"Out of suffering have emerged the strongest souls;
the most massive characters are seared with scars."
—Kahlil Gibran

The truth is, beauty is glorified but scars are frowned on. That position is taken from a place of poverty. One of my definition of poverty is, "the inability or failure to convert resources into meaningful means." Both beauty and scars are endowed with wealth, some realized, while others are waiting to be uncovered. In this chapter, the emphasis is the wealth and beauty of scars.

But Thomas, one of the twelve, called Didymus, was not with them when Jesus came. The other disciples therefore said unto him, We have seen the Lord. But he said unto them, Except I shall see in his hands the print of the nails, and put my finger into the print of the nails, and thrust my hand into his side, I will not believe. And after eight days again his disciples were within, and Thomas with them: then came Jesus, the doors being shut, and stood in the midst, and said, Peace be unto you. Then saith he to Thomas, Reach hither thy finger, and behold my hands; and reach hither thy hand, and thrust it into my side: and be not faithless, but believing. And Thomas answered and said unto him, My Lord and my God. Jesus saith unto him, Thomas, because thou hast seen me, thou hast believed: blessed are they that have not seen, and yet have believed (John 20:24-29).

Thomas refused to believe until he saw the scars. Stop being ashamed of your scars, they tell your story. Wear your scars proudly. They are testifying loudly. They say, you are not a quitter, you went through the fire and the flood and made it. You did not give in to the encouragement to commit suicide. You are more than conquerors. Please don't silence your scars.

There was a time when persons did not talk about things like being raped. But there is a new generation who understands that they are not a slave to the evil that was done to them. Today, they openly share their scars as a means of encouraging someone and glorifying God. You cannot talk about the mess until you have gotten over it. Satan can no longer keep you silent. Don't allow anyone to bind your present and future to your past mess. Your steps are ordered by God, not by the events of your SCARS. Understand that the enemy got wind of your mess and tried to expose it with the intent of destroying you. But he did not know that your mess would have become your message.

Here is your breakthrough. Stop trying to cover or hide your scars. It's actually giving Satan ammunition to be used against you. Refuse to give Satan secrets on you. Listen, I love what Jesus said, "He that is without sin among you, let him first cast a stone at her" (John 8:7b). Stones were dropped to the ground as persons examined themselves quickly and shamefully. We tend to enjoy highlighting a person's errors because it somehow helps us to not see ours.

The struggles are real. We go to church, sing a few songs, worship and listen to a message, and then go back home to face all the struggles there. It is sad that the places like church and home, where we are supposed to be ourselves, because of the scars, we often-times wear a mask. Some persons have worn their masks for so long, presently they don't remember their true self. The fear of exposing who you are on the inside cripples you to reside behind the mask while hiding your scars, which are your wealth. God can fix the internal battles that arise from your scars better than any person can!

Before "John" became a child of God, his hobby was fornication. God saved him and he was instantaneously delivered. But Satan crept in and deceived him. He told him, fornication is wrong, but not masturbation. Masturbation was the way to relieve himself without sinning. He believed and began masturbating. Then there was a war to stop after he discovered he was deceived. The battle was won. Now, he is a counsellor and minister who helps persons struggling with masturbation and sexual sins. He went through his mess and after all the thorns, there is beauty. The thorn is what brings us to the next level. The thorns are positioned to disrupt your comfort and make you look higher.

As we renew our minds, be certain to grasp this concept: *you were chosen to wear your scars.* Your scars are your testimony that you came back from the war. No, you did not die on the battlefield. Your scars validate who you say you are. Kahlil Gibran, author of "The Prophet" which has been translated into over 100 different languages, making it one of the most translated books in history said, *"Out of suffering have emerged the strongest souls; the most massive characters are seared with scars."* Your scars identify you as one who did not quit. You knew the blades that awaited you, and you braved the road. You see your scars as disabilities, but let them become your platform of motivation. You can find your purpose out of your pain, ridicule, and indifference. The time you spend trying to fit in and resemble the societal dictated norms, you should pursue a degree in accepting who you are and finding your life's purpose and destiny.

Many persons die without knowing and fulfilling their divine purpose because they choose to live in another's shadow. Whose life are you living? Yours or your friends'? The pursuit of happiness through the shadow of another will result in self-destruction. Don't deprive the world of knowing your uniqueness. Your scars distinguish and separate you. Embrace them. You can chose to exist with your scars or live and enjoy the wealth of the same.

What has rendered you disabled? Come on, you can be what God ordained you to be. Your ordination was decided before you were scarred and will not become nullified because you have been branded. When there are challenges, address them. Overcome them. Don't quit because of the bumpy road. Get a 4x4 Jeep. Someone needs to hear this. In your scars lies your purpose and wealth. Stop complaining and embrace your uniqueness as given by the Lord.

Each new chapter of your life will merely be a repetition of the previous unless you make some serious Mind Renewal adjustments. Let the new be constituted by the changes you will make. Decide to live not just exist, pursue your dreams. If you abandoned your calling, resume the journey. Work on your health, family life, education, relationship with God (first) and stop hiding your scars. Your scars are God's gift to you.

Men might be afraid to use the disqualified, that is, the ones with the horrible history. The ones who have to give censored testimonies, but God has always used such people. For example, murderer Moses, adulterous David, deceiver Jacob, me and you WITH OUR SCARS.

MASTER YOUR RESPONSE

A harsh reality is that not everyone can handle your scars and subsequently, they are blinded to their beauty. As you purpose to be proud of your scars, be conscious that you will receive mixed feedback.

As a teenager, I struggled with low self-esteem which affected my performance in high school. My Principles of Business (P.O.B.) teacher told me, I would not amount to anything. That was harsh but not enough to sink me. It hit hard but an inner fighter was pulled to the forefront. Therefore, I used it as a motivation to pursue passes. I became driven to prove that I'm not what she said. I sat the exam, got the results and searched for her to show her my pass. Negative words spoken can either break or make you. You decide how the matter unfolds. You either allow the abuse to be the nail that seals your coffin or the dirt you step on to climb out of the hole. You decide!

In the account of 2 Kings, Chapter 5, we see the mastery of one's response at its greatest demonstration. There was a slave girl, one who was taken from her home country and forced into a secondary status, as a matter of fact, no status. Slaves had no say. But she knew the answer to her captive's problem. He had leprosy. Naaman, the one who captured her, who burned her city and enslaved her, needed help.

She knew the answer. Here was the crossroad. After all the wrongs he had done to her family and city, does he deserve her help? She knew if he only got to the prophet, he would be made whole. It can be very challenging, looking beyond the past evil to help in the present. In renewing our minds, we must be intentional in not withholding knowledge, truth, prayer, forgiveness, and love even to those who have and are doing us wrong.

She demonstrated the power of not allowing the wrongs done to her to further enslave her. Subjecting yourself to the dictates of past hurts and pains block you from receiving the wealth of forgiveness and love. She was physically enslaved but she was spiritually free. She told her captor where to get help and he was healed. Are you free today? In ascertaining your status, you can look at your responses to correction, rebuke or guidance which is different from your own ideology.

This was a slave girl. There is no name mentioned or age, but what is mentioned is her demonstration of forgivingness and love.... She evangelized through love. She was at her place of work without pay. We must ensure at work that our co-workers see the love radiating from us. If not, no amount of invitations will get them to come to church. Let love be your tool of evangelism.

Please learn this Mind Renewal truth from this slave girl: *you should never feel because you are not known/recognized, that God by His divine plan will not use you.* He'll allow you to be in the right place with the right people and the right time for His glory to be revealed. Very often persons bow to the notion, that because they don't "have the thermometers behind their names," not riding with the "right crowd" or from the "right family" that they are not valuable. But God uses people with issues who are available and have a pure heart. Those are the ones God uses because they realize to whom much is given much is required.

CRITICISM

A major sore is our response to criticisms. According to Connor Grooms, there are two types of criticism: constructive criticism and projected criticism. Constructive criticism is the type of criticism that every great person seeks out. Projected criticism is an emotional, negative reaction to something you've said or done. Renew your mind with this truth, "Your response to criticism determines your way forward." Let's look at an example of this with the University of the West Indies in addressing a Gleaner Editors' Forum.

University of the West Indies principal, Professor Archibald McDonald, said while the label, "intellectual ghetto" hurt badly, it also served as a motivator to the faculty at the Mona campus. 'It hurt our feelings, but it didn't really damage us. What it really did was to stimulate us to reflect and look at the work of the university, and we responded,' said McDonald of the term coined by one of Jamaica's leading journalists, Wilmot 'Motty' Perkins, who died five years ago. 'We responded in more ways than one, and if you look at it today, the university is now closer to the Jamaican society than it ever was,' added McDonald.

He accepted that there was a need for revival in some areas, telling *Gleaner* editors and reporters that there were criticisms about the relevance or irrelevance of some courses offered. According to McDonald, a concerted effort has since been placed on renewal.

We responded to the criticisms, including that of Mr. Perkins. We have been criticized for other things, including that our programmes are irrelevant. And the response is to introduce programmes that are beneficial to the Jamaican society. Programmes such as dentistry were introduced because although there is a dental school in Trinidad, it can't supply the number of dentists that a country like Jamaica needs.

MORE THAN RESPONSE TO CRITICISM

Citing a transformation of the science and technology programmes, McDonald said engineering studies has not only been a response to criticism about relevance but a desire by the university to attract more male students. As a result, a noticeable increase in the number of males has been recorded in some programmes.

At one time, we had less than 25 percent males enrolled in the university. By transforming the programmes, rather than just pure physics or pure chemistry, we have engineering and computing which attract more males, which is still not where we want it to be, but it has now increased to 33 percent.

So criticisms like that from Mr. Perkins, if you take an open-minded approach, you use it to improve on it and we did. We welcome constructive criticisms because what that does for us is to put things in perspective and, rather than us looking from inside, it may be a view that will help us to improve,' said the university principal.

McDonald was supported by senior lecturer in the Department of Life Sciences, Professor Mona Webber, who believed that much of the criticism from Perkins was because the university did not do a good job of promoting itself.

'We don't let people know about what we are doing. So we have redesigned and reconfigured and restructured. But this expansion of our Research Day shows the importance of engagement and gives us an oppor-tunity to showcase to the Jamaican society what we are doing. So we are not seen as this elitist institution, which is really because of a lack of knowledge by the wider society about what we are doing,' said Webber.

The university's response made the difference. They took the negative battering from a popular radio personality and converted it for their prosperity. Rather than seeing the person as being a hater, they took his criticism as a guide to the needed transform-ation and forward movement of the school. They were driven to redesign, reconfigure, and restructure the school's operations. They looked at the relevance and irrelevance of their programs. The university is now at a better place because it chose to let the criti-cism work for them. As you renew your mind, let cri-ticism work for you. The truth sometimes hurts, but it's better than soothing lies.

My years in high school did not afford me a lot of uniforms, some days I had to repeat. One day a fellow student said to me, "Leostone, you are smelling mouldy." I felt embarrassed. I left school went home and washed my uniforms. That was the last day I wore a dirty uniform to school. Years later, I saw the same student and thanked her. Those harsh words were the truth and they helped me.

While there are tremendous benefits to constructive criticisms, the first challenge we face is the conversion of negative criticism to constructive criticism. This con-version begins in your mind, process it. Let us invest in the development of the necessary skill of making all

things work together for our good. This includes negative criticisms armed with daggers to kill confidence
and destiny. I've always promoted this truth, you don't
have control over what is said to you, but you have
power over your response. You can decide to surrender your power to a seemingly attacker by allowing
their words or actions to cripple you, or you can
choose to use the negatives as ingredients for growth.

As you renew your mind, you must decide if the
negatives cast against you will serve as the tune to
your funeral procession, or the rhythm of your new
awakening. The decision is yours.

The benefits of criticisms are too rich for us to not
capture and utilize. Criticism can promote personal
growth of an individual, union, organization and even a
nation. It challenges you to step outside of the box,
which is the norm, the expected or average. Criticism
can be that needed push start that you are searching or
hoping for. What if you see your critics as necessary
engines to move you from ordinary to your maximum
potential? We would then agree that they are strategically placed to have us not settle where we would not
stand out as different or relevant. In so doing we
stumble upon another benefit: improved relationships.

Criticism gives us the chance to see others in a different light. Knowing that someone may just be trying
to help us improve gives us a greater appreciation for
the relationship we share. Renew your mind with this
truth, *critique me till I matriculate to a better me.*

Criticism, if received properly, can make one stronger.
The university's actions validated this position. It grew
in strength and saw an increase in enrolment of males.

Before a car is released to the market, it undergoes various tests of strength and durability. This includes speed, efficiency and crashes. From these tests, adjustments are made until the vehicle is at a standard that is strong and acceptable. Criticism shows that you are human. We all have flaws as human beings and receiving criticism highlights our imperfections. Rather than caving under the weight of our shortcomings being made known, let us strive to improve our weak areas without beating down ourselves. Please understand as long as life permits, there will be room for self-improvement. You will never attain the status of no room for self-improvement.

Criticisms help us to recognize the areas we need to progress. It also serves as a self-confidence building tool. When I was criticized by my schoolmate, it pushed me to make necessary changes. My self-confidence grew knowing that I was clean and smelling good. A transformation took place. I became more involved and open to being involved.

The emotional benefit must never be ignored. An emotionally unstable person is like a ticking bomb waiting to detonate. Being able to appreciate criticism sets one in the position not to react but to evaluate. Not retaliating at someone for what they said gives us the chance to look into how it affects us emotionally. This examination can be a guide to our forward actions or utterances.

The traditional attitude towards criticisms is unhealthy and unproductive. As we renew our minds, instead of being in locked mode, let us accept criticisms as keys to unlocking different approaches and possibilities. Be open to new ideas and strategies especially if the originally held ones are not producing or have maximized their potential. Criticism gives us the opportunity to open up to new ideas that we might not have even considered. Let us adopt this position, if you love me, critique me until I'm my best me.

MIND RENEWAL KEYS

In this chapter on "Beauty of Scars" we have shared some Mind Renewal keys to help you to become a better person. Here is a summary of these keys that you can apply to your life daily or as the circumstances arise. Read and meditate on them. Then implement as become necessary.

1. Poverty is "the inability or failure to convert resources into meaningful means."
2. Stop being ashamed of your scars, they tell your story.
3. Your steps are ordered by God, not by the events of your SCARS.
4. You were chosen to wear your scars, they validate and express the unique you.

5. Let your scars become your platform of motivation. In them abide your purpose and wealth.

6. The pursuit of happiness through the shadow of another will result in self-destruction.

7. What you have control of is your response. It determines your way forward.

8. Let criticism work for you. Extract your potential prosperity from the intended negativity.

9. You will never attain the status of no room for self-improvement.

10. Adopt this position: if you love me, critique me until I'm my best me.

CHAPTER 15:

YOUR NEXT

"Insanity is doing the same thing repeatedly but expecting a different result." —Albert Einstein

I was raised in poverty: no electricity, no running water, zinc bathroom and kitchen. I played barefooted and wore one pair of shoes to church every Sunday. I carried water to fill a drum from the standpipe. The latrine toilet had to be polished every Saturday. I collected firewood for cooking from nearby woodlands. I saw and knew my present but my *Next* evaded me. My Next engulfed with abundance, favour and prosperity was there but hidden.

In the English language, there are commas and full stops. Each commands a pause or a stop. When a comma is seen, you know for a certainty that a *Next* is at hand. When a full stop is used, sometimes it's a continuation or completion. The word "next" speaks to the continuation. The fact that you are reading this message today means you have a *Next*. Your Next might be: your next husband, next job, next church, next million, next baby, next car, next season, next level, next disappointment, next storm, next rejection etc.

HOW TO BE SUCCESSFUL IN YOUR NEXT

To receive and embrace your God-designed *Next*, you will have opposition. The greater your *Next*, the greater the opposition... This opposition while predominantly seen in the physical, is orchestrated in the spiritual domain by spiritual wickedness. The phrase spiritual wickedness in high places refers to Satan and his demonic horde that inhabit the spiritual realm. This is a world unseen by us that exists in our midst. These spirit beings are not friendly toward us and will use every opportunity they can find to torment us. Sometimes they plant lies in our minds that contradict the truth we learn from God.

Spiritual wickedness targets the individual through lies and deception with the intent of having persons live below their God-given location. We live in fear of going forward because we were hurt in the past, when the future is loaded with favour and blessings. The battle is in our minds. Many persons have lived lies for so long that they no longer know the truth. I met a beautiful young lady in 2010, who had not looked in a mirror for a while because she believed she was unattractive. It was painful to see her suffer. She believed a lie. Lies planted by these spirits, serve to divert, derail and abort our *Next*.

There is no need to be dismayed. The Apostle Paul said we have divine weapons to take these thoughts captive and make them obedient to Christ (2 Cor. 10:3-5). You are equipped with the relevant tools to secure your victorious *Next*.

LETTING GO OF THE LOSS

You will never receive what is in store for you until you let go what you have lost. The temptation of believing that you have experienced or lived your best has the potential to hold you in bondage for as long as you allow it. Here lies your deliverance: *your best days are still to be lived.* Yesterday was good. Today is great but tomorrow shall be your greatest! Yesterday was the foundation years. No one lives in the foundation of a building. The old hymn says, "Better days are coming." Refusing to let go of the loss, is like deciding not to live tomorrow. The account of Genesis 19:17-26 supports the above position.

> And it came to pass, when they had brought them forth abroad, that he said, Escape for thy life; look not behind thee, neither stay thou in all the plain; escape to the mountain, lest thou be consumed. And Lot said unto them, Oh, not so, my Lord: Behold now, thy servant hath found grace in thy sight, and thou hast magnified thy mercy, which thou hast shewed unto me in saving my life; and I cannot escape to the mountain, lest some evil take me, and I die: Behold now, this city is near to flee unto, and it is a little one: Oh, let me escape thither, (is it not a little one?) and my soul shall

live. And he said unto him, See, I have accepted thee concerning this thing also, that I will not overthrow this city, for the which thou hast spoken. Haste thee, escape thither; for I cannot do anything till thou be come thither. Therefore the name of the city was called Zoar. The sun was risen upon the earth when Lot entered into Zoar. Then the Lord rained upon Sodom and upon Gomorrah brimstone and fire from the Lord out of heaven; And he overthrew those cities, and all the plain, and all the inhabitants of the cities, and that which grew upon the ground. But his wife looked back from behind him, and she became a pillar of salt (Genesis 19:17-26).

Her heart and eyes looked back to where she was coming from. She knew the past but not the future of uncertainty. However, the depth of what the Lord spoke was not about the physical or geographical, but it extended to her state of mind and spirit. She was positioned and en-route to safety, being delivered, but her heart returned to the place where God had closed to them. The place that was closed was one of mixed happenings. On one hand it was full of laughter, provisions, friends and accumulation of assets. On the other hand, it was filled with pain, hatred, deception, loneliness, tears, poverty and destruction. Your present situation and thoughts may be dragging you back to where you were, but God has better for you.

Not every closed door is demonic. God closes doors to keep some out and to keep some within. Thank you God, for the closure and the new direction! If the past was the best, God would have kept it together. Understand, the job you lost, the relationship that broke or the church at which you were victimized was not God's best.

There is a song that says "my body is here but my mind is on the other side of town," that is the essence of this dialogue. Where are your thoughts and your spirit? Are you at the place of God's will or are you at the place where God has closed? Oftentimes, we focus on the physical but not the mental and the spiritual. Are you in bed with your spouse but thinking of another person? Do you long to be touched by a former lover? Do you still dream of that person to whom you gave your heart as a teenager? Do you still reminisce with gladness, the joys of your life of sin? I love the line of the song "Reprise" which says, "I can't go back. I won't go back to the way it used to be before your presence came and changed me." Let us be resolute, we are not getting stuck or going back into our past. We are letting go of the losses and moving forward into our "Next." Lot's wife needed to make a transition from knowledge to faith and she failed. What she knew and was instructed to leave behind was knowledge. What she was instructed to pursue by faith was her *Next*. However, she killed her *Next*.

LIGHTENING THE LOAD

As we proceed into our next, let us begin with lightening our loads. Sometimes with good intentions, we stretch ourselves so thin we become of no effect. We must endeavour to stop bombarding ourselves with every care that presents itself. Years ago, I was asked if there is any "no" in my mouth. The following might sound harsh but I had to learn it. It's okay to say, "No." Not just saying no, but accepting no also. We struggle with the feeling that we have been rejected. But the truth is, what is a priority to you is not necessarily a priority to someone else. Pastor David Grant once said, "Not because something is a priority to someone, means it must be yours also." We will not always get what we want. In lightening your load, you must leave room for the best by saying no to the good. The good has the potential to deceive you into believing that you have arrived at your pinnacle, while the best stares at you with desire.

Every four years we find our eyes glued to a projecting screen as we watch our favourite athletes do their craft at the Olympics. My most watched competition is track and field. What is noticeable is the scanty dressing that is displayed. No heavy training gears or equipment. They understand, they will be going fast, and against the competition. In renewing our minds we must run light as seen in Hebrews 12:1.

Wherefore seeing we also are compassed about with so great a cloud of witnesses, let us lay aside every weight, and the sin which doth so easily beset us, and let us run with patience the race that is set before us (Hebrews 12:1).

Weights are hindering our ability to run and causing us to experience spiritual shortness of breath, tiredness and pulled muscles. We must, remove from our life everything and everyone that will hinder us from running the ultimate race of eternal life that is set before us. For this to be accomplished, you must run each Next light. The truth is many of us today have struggled with letting go of things/people in this life whom we believe we cannot live without. Sadly some of these people/things that we hold on to are holding us back from maximizing our Next and fulfilling our purpose.

This is a common struggle among children of God especially in today's age where there has been an increase in distractions within the world. We must embrace that place of separation. Going forward, we must analyze our lives. Think about the adjustments that can be made and the weights that can be laid aside in order to run the race that is set before us. We don't want to merely run the race but run effectively. Be cognizant of this truth, each Next is like small races which leads to the main race of eternal life.

In our pursuit to drop the weights, we must consider the spiritual weights. The soul ties, the blood covenant relationships that we still carry after 10 years of physical separation, and the weight of being in the wrong assignment. Is the job you are doing a weight or an assignment? Are we spiritually cleared to function in that capacity? There is a weight that many of us have that we pretend is not there. It is resentment of our parents and church leaders. 1 John 4:20b says, "for he that loveth not his brother whom he hath seen, how can he love God whom he hath not seen?" How can we resent or detest our earthly parents, both physical and spiritual and say we love God? If you stand guilty, this is a weight you need to be lightened of.

Favoritism is also a weight we walk around with. In a family of several siblings, the mother, a devout Christian was accused of favouring one child over the others. Her defence was, "Jesus had favourites too." We base our favouritism on educational background, religion, skin tone or beauty but what we miss is that we are all equal in God's sight. As we pursue Mind Renewal, let us begin to see through the lenses of our Maker. Equality is not a gift it's a right. As you lighten the weight in pursuit of the renewal of your mind, understand that persons are different. Rather than preferring one over another, appreciate their individuality and differences.

ACKNOWLEDGING ERRORS OF THE PAST

If you are going to be successful in your *Next*, you must look at the errors you made in the past and make the changes needed. Yes, my sister, my brother, changes are needed. Albert Einstein is credited with the quote, "insanity is doing the same thing repeatedly but expecting a different result." Employing the same attitude and actions of the past, will produce the same results in the present and future. For too long we have looked at the errors of others and what they have done, but refusing to deeply examine ourselves. We are only defeating ourselves when we refuse to acknowledge that we contributed to our past failures. As you renew your mind going into your next, know this: nothing changed, nothing new experienced. Newness is hidden in abundance behind the known.

BE YOUR OWN CUPBEARER

Bishop TD Jakes spoke about three types of people, confidants, comrades and constituents. Confidants are few, these are the ones who are into you, whether you are in trouble or not. These tell you when you are right or wrong. Constituents are in greater quantity. They are not into you but what you are into. As long as you are in what they are into, they will ride with you. If someone comes along who is able to further their agenda, they will leave you.

Comrades are the persons who are not for you but are against what you are against. They might not even like you but hate what you hate. They are not with you! As you renew your mind, don't be fooled: agreement does not always equate togetherness. Please note, failure to properly categorize the people who are frequent in your life, is recipe for disaster. Think about the devastation of treating a comrade as confidant. A wrongly labeled close comrade can be worse than an open enemy. Each category of persons must remain in their circle of description.

Comrades are at the outer circle, constituents at the circle and the confidants at the inner circle. Your inner circle will be very small. Renew your mind in this wise; it's easier for the person who is close to you to harm you than the one that is kept far. Bob Marley in one of his songs says "only your friend knows your secret, only he can reveal it." This is nothing new. The kings of old knew this and employed the services of cupbearers. According to the International Standard Encyclopedia, a cupbearer is:

An officer of high rank at ancient oriental courts, whose duty it was to serve the wine at the king's table. On account of the constant fear of plots and intrigues, a person must be regarded as thoroughly trustworthy to hold this position. He must guard against poison in the king's cup, and was sometimes required to swallow some of the wine before serving it.

You are your own cupbearer. Pay close attention to those you allow in our close proximity. Let's look at Matthew 26:47-50:

And while he yet spake, lo, Judas, one of the twelve, came, and with him a great multitude with swords and staves, from the chief priests and elders of the people. Now he that betrayed him gave them a sign, saying, 'Whomsoever I shall kiss, that same is he: hold him fast.' And forthwith he came to Jesus, and said, Hail, master; and kissed him. And Jesus said unto him, 'Friend, wherefore art thou come?' Then came they, and laid hands on Jesus, and took him (Matthew 26:47-50).

As you enter into the *Next* of your life, be careful not to believe every smile, laughter, kiss, or handshake is friendly and mean you well. Be conscious, the new job or husband might have been someone's prayer request. As Christians, we are too trusting. 1 John 1:1 warns against it. We are to try every spirit. We blunder by sharing our story with everyone, stop it. In this, your *Next,* apply wisdom. Learning how to do that is hard at times but we have to ask the Holy Spirit for wisdom. Be confident that not everyone around us has good intentions. We just have to talk less and show them the results. God will provide that individual in whom you can confide. It might just be a stranger.

The blessings of your *Next* will cause you to gain and lose some friends. Your Next is so compact, even present friends will not be able to celebrate with you. Your elevation will unveil hidden envy in the hearts of some present family and friends. If we pay close attention, we will see that the smile changes. Notice the infrequency of the phone calls. Notice Jesus said to Judas, "a friend betrays me with a kiss." Jesus referred to him despite his evil act as a friend. In your Next, don't allow a person's evil doings to convert you into becoming bitter. Renew your mind with this truth, *don't let bitterness take your glory.*

SCALING DOWN

You dare not believe everyone you carried in the before, must accompany you in the *Next*. There will be the necessity of scaling down. Let's examine Acts 15:36-40:

And some days after Paul said unto Barnabas, Let us go again and visit our brethren in every city where we have preached the word of the LORD, and see how they do. And Barnabas determined to take with them John, whose surname was Mark. But Paul thought not good to take him with them, who departed from them from Pamphylia, and went not with them to the work. And the contention was so sharp between them, that they departed asunder one from the other: and so Barnabas took Mark, and sailed unto Cyprus; And Paul chose Silas, and departed, being recommended by the brethren unto the grace of God (Acts 15:36-40).

Barnabas wanted to take Mark with them but Paul disagreed. Paul thought Mark was not a good candidate because he had deserted them before. Paul was adamant, "for my *Next* Mark has not proven himself worthy to carry." This is a deep renewal of mind. Even though it hurts, we have to release, forgive and move on. The hardest to leave behind are those who are good to you. They had your back, prayed with you and gave guidance. However, they are still not a part of your *Next*.

Looking in the technological arena, we come across floppy discs which were invented in 1967. Today floppy discs are no longer used. The younger generation is not familiar with this storage mechanism. The Floppy Disc served well in its era, but became extinct. Be very certain that not everything that served you well must be taken into your *Next*. As you renew your mind, be aware that not everyone comes into your life with a "no expiry" date. Some persons come for seasons or periods. There are persons who support you now, who have been holding you up from step one but cannot join you in your *Next*. And not only can't accompany you but just can't get any information on it. Begin to pray. Ask God to reveal to you those who are a part of your Next.

BRACE FOR NEGATIVE FEEDBACK

We learn a powerful lesson for our *Next* from Nehemiah, you don't need to publicize your *Next* move. Let's look at Nehemiah 2:12-16.

And I arose in the night, I and some few men with me; neither told I any man what my God had put in my heart to do at Jerusalem: neither was there any beast with me, save the beast that I rode upon. And I went out by night by the gate of the valley, even before the dragon well, and to the dung port, and viewed the walls of Jerusalem, which were broken down, and the gates thereof were consumed with fire. Then I went on to the gate of the fountain, and to the king's pool: but there was no place for the beast that was under me to pass. Then went I up in the night by the brook, and viewed the wall, and turned back, and entered by the gate of the valley, and so returned. And the rulers knew not whither I went, or what I did; neither had I as yet told it to the Jews, nor to the priests, nor to the nobles, nor to the rulers, nor to the rest that did the work (Nehemiah 2:12-16).

The rulers were positioned to assist him. He was the visionary carrier of the dream. However, he knew you must ensure your mouth is not operating on diarrhea. Lord, give us spiritual warm salt water or pepto bismol. If you are working on a small business and every time you relate it to friends, it's like it goes back to step one, realize God wants you to shut your mouth. Only He should know your next move. As a child growing up, my mother had a plaque on the wall that said, "Lord help me to keep my big mouth shut." Your thoughts are so valuable, God hid them from the outside world. They are the most secured element of a human. Renew your mind in this wise, *an open mouth exposes your mind, exposure attracts based on the content being exposed.*

Be selective in who or what you attract by your ex-pressed thoughts.

Brace for negative feedback but never apologize for the blessing of the Lord upon your life. You've got to go to your NEXT! Truth is, some persons cannot handle your plans and aspirations. They sometimes are scared of you and your vision. If you love your family and friends, you should not burden them with what they are not equipped to handle your dreams and visions.

In 1 Kings 13, God told the young prophet to go speak to the king and the Lord commanded him not to eat or drink but deliver the message and go. But the older prophet heard of what was done, and went and told the young prophet that the Lord told him to tell him to come and eat and drink with him. He lied to the younger prophet and because the younger prophet disobeyed God, he did not make it back home. He was killed on his way.

In your Next, you will come across some lying spirit that does not like what God is doing through you. But they do not know of the sacrifice you made to be where you are in God. And because they are your des-tiny killer, they will come like wolves in sheep clothing. You need spiritual eyes to discern them for they come and they come good. But they do not mean you any good. They are liars and manipulators, who want to turn you from the will of God and then laugh at you. They are everywhere, including the church. They talk the talk and walk the walk, and go by all sorts of big titles. Be careful in your Next who you listen to. A lying spirit once told me a lie which caused me to invest and lose money. Lies are designed to sound like truth.

CHANGE YOUR EXPECTATIONS

In your *Next,* a necessary mind renewal is: *increase your level of request to God.* You have been asking too small. When I studied at the Jamaica Theological Seminary, I saw a lecturer with a very nice projector. I enquired of the cost and when he told me the exorbitant price, I responded, "That's too much for me." The lecturer profoundly said, "That depends on the size of your God." You will never function outside of the parameters of your faith. If you see Him as a small God, with small capabilities, then you will never require anything big of Him. The requests that you make of Him, testify of your faith conviction

Your request reflects your faith. It's time for your faith to grow. As your faith grows, your expectations also grow. If you are reading this and walking with an expectation to fail, God wants you to stop. You may have experienced failure so frequently that you have come to expect failure. Stop making failure your surroundings.

You need a spiritual mentor. Fast and ask God to connect you to Destiny Helpers. One manifestation of an anointed man or woman of God is their ability and willingness to submit to leadership, correction, and teaching. They employ quick forgiveness and obedience. God wants someone to know, your Next is better, brighter, lighter and richer. Things you fought and struggled with in the past and present, you will not struggle with in the future.

In Mathew chapter 15, we see a mother refusing to be ignored or pushed aside. She wanted her daughter's life changed. Her daughter needed healing and she refused to take no for an answer. The mother with the sick daughter could have turned away because she was insulted by Jesus. But she pressed into her Next. Be desperate to walk into and receive all victory in your Next. You have to be fervent. There is no place for being thin-skinned in this your Next. Declare that this Next is your winning season. Everything attached to you will win and prosper in Jesus' mighty name!

Recently, the Holy Spirit said, "you are about to be challenged." This meant I was positioned to go to a next level. That growth that I have been praying for, cried for and desired is at hand. Your Next might not be a walk in the park. Are you ready for your Next?

MIND RENEWAL KEYS

In this chapter on "Your Next" we have shared some Mind Renewal keys to help you to become a better person. Here is a summary of these keys that you can apply to your life daily or as the circumstances arise. Read and meditate on them. Pray and declare them over your life to walk in the victory God has prepared for you.

1. The greater your Next, the greater the opposition.
2. You will never receive what is in store for you until you let go what you have lost.
3. Your best days are still to be lived.
4. Not every closed door is demonic.
5. Leave room for the best by saying no to the good.
6. Nothing changed, nothing new experienced. Newness is hidden in abundance beyond the known.
7. Agreement does not always equate to togetherness.
8. Do not believe every smile, laughter, kiss, or handshake is friendly and mean you well.
9. Talk less but show the results.
10. God will provide that individual in whom you can confide. It might just be a stranger.
11. Your elevation will unveil hidden envy in the hearts of some present family and friends.
12. Don't let bitterness take your glory.
13. Not everyone comes into your life with a "no expiry" date. Some persons come for seasons or periods.
14. An open mouth exposes your mind, exposure attracts based on the content being exposed.
15. Brace for negative feedback. But never apologize for the blessing of the Lord upon your life.
16. Demonstrate love by not burdening family and friends with your dreams and visions.
17. Expect negative feedback.
18. Ensure your mouth is not operating on diarrhea.

19. New challenges can be a sign of near new blessings.

CHAPTER 16:

MARAH TO ELIM

"Make your pain your propelling agent."

—Leostone Morrison

The children of Israel journeyed from the place of bondage to the promised land of freedom and abundance. However, it was not without challenges and setbacks. One challenge encountered was recorded in Exodus 15:22b-25.

And they went three days in the wilderness and found no water. And when they came to Marah, they could not drink of the waters of Marah, for they were bitter: therefore the name of it was called Marah. And the people murmured against Moses, saying, what shall we drink? And he cried unto the Lord; and the Lord shewed him a tree, which when he had cast into the waters, the waters were made sweet: there he made for them a statute and an ordinance, and there he proved them (Exodus 15:22b-25).

Let's extract some Mind Renewal keys from the above mentioned passage.

1. GOD HAS THE ANSWER

Can we shift our attitude from believing that we have the answers or the answers must come from us? The truth is, we don't have the answers. God has the answers. The people cried unto their leader Moses, "we need water to drink." As you renew your mind, please be specific in your asking. Water was found in Marah. Therefore, water was not the problem. The condition or the state of the water was the issue. Renew your mind with this truth, don't be beguiled, not every provision equates to solution. Moses did not say, "Let's go back to the Red Sea for water." Let's stay right here a bit.

Don't return to where God delivered you from. You got separated from your husband/wife, your job etc., and you are facing hard times, don't go back begging, press on. Hear this: lack, insufficiency and poverty can be idols because the mindset has been elevated above the Word and knowledge of who God is.

The provision for you is nearer than you think. You must have a made up mind like the woman with the issue of blood recorded in Mathew 9:21. She said, "if I could just touch the hem of His garment, I know (not maybe) I shall be made whole." That's the renewed mind we need to implement. Replace the maybe attitude with that of assurance, certainty. I know God is my answer.

The woman with the issue of blood was not alone in being steadfast in conviction. In Daniel chapter 3, King Nebuchadnezzar made a golden statue and ordered everyone in the province to bow to it. Three Hebrew boys—Shadrach, Meshach and Abednego—refused to bow. They only bowed to Jehovah God. The king in his fury threatened to throw them in the fire if they did not comply with his demands. The Hebrew boys said, " oh king we are not careful to answer you in this wise, but we know our God will deliver us out of your hands, and if He chooses not to, we are still not bowing to your statue." Don't bow! Don't bow to the system of the world or the demands of evil. Don't bow to the pressure of wants and needs. Moses in responding to the people's cry, cried unto God. It was God who sent Moses. Therefore, go back to God. Well done Moses! Remember how the journey began. Stay with the source.

2. THE ANSWER MIGHT NOT BE CONVENTIONAL

Warning! Stop trying to dictate to God how you want it done! Stop using the scripture "the Lord grants the desires of our hearts" (Psalm 37:4) to justify you trying to bully God. Read again, God will grant the desires of your heart if you delight in Him. So God will not kill your ex-wife/ex-husband because you desire it. An easy or more conventional water provision would be to send rain, but that's not God. He's spectacular, uncommon, and there is nothing ordinary about Him. When He does it, everyone knows He did it.

God showed Moses a tree. Please pay attention when God is speaking. He speaks in different ways. He speaks through His Word (the Bible), audibly, through songs, signs, nature, dreams, visions etc. However, when He speaks to you, listen. Sometimes we are praying about things God has already spoken to us about. God showed Moses a tree. He cast it into the water and the bitterness left, it became sweet. Pay attention. The name of the tree was not given. Meaning, by itself this tree had no medicinal properties. There is nothing special about it but when used by God that changes. Never underestimate those who are around you. Your Destiny Helpers might not come with titles and prestige. Might be a no-name little boy with his fish and bread. Never forget, God does not see as how men see. Therefore, God's answers are not bound to being conventional.

This teaching is dear to me, as I have lived it. Being placed in the insignificant circle because of poverty (financial) and seeing the turn around by Jesus. I owe praise to no man, save my God. He did it, over and over again. Look what the Lord has done. I'm not ashamed of my past and you should not be either. God has transformed you. You are no longer a nameless tree in the place of Marah (bitterness).

God knows how to change a *nobody* into a *somebody*. Stop seeing yourself as insignificant. That chapter of your life ended abruptly when Jesus came into your heart. Your death to sin drowned insignificance. You are more than how you or others see you. They see a clerk, but God sees the person who is causing the company to be blessed. They see a pastor, God sees a revolutionary. This mind renewal strength needs repeating. See yourself from the lenses of God.

Unfortunately, we have been suffering from the wrong focus. We have been focusing on the deficiencies, problems, our own capabilities, and inadequacies. God wants us to be victorious. The remedy for the feeling of inadequacy is to magnify God above everything. It's one thing to be nameless, but to be nameless in Marah is another story. God is the story changer. The Lord wants you to know, where you are now, might be new for you but this is not your preferred environment. Keep trusting God. He is not limited to space, location or time. He's not going to show up, He's already there. He has you where you are because He wants to bless you and use you in the presence of your enemies. The enemy saw you as insignificant, but as you obey God, they will know there is nothing insignificant about you.

Think about the opposition you got, was there anything insignificant about them? How then can you be insignificant? I heard the Holy Spirit say, "you think you were insignificant, that's how serious the warfare got, but you are not." Your warfare is not normal. The rejection from family, friends, neighbours, husband, wife, is nothing normal. When you have wisdom about who you are in the warfare you operate as victors. You are not insignificant.

3. PAIN—YOUR PROPELLING AGENT

Hear what the Holy Spirit says, "you see pain, God sees launching pad." Your pain is your propelling agent. If the water had not been bitter, that tree would not have been used. The purpose of the tree would not have been realized. Pain connects you to your Destiny Helpers. As loud as you can, shout: "I'm not insignificant." Your pain is not insignificant. It was good that you were afflicted, rejected, persecuted, abandoned, divorced, sidelined etc. The value of freedom is not known until challenged with oppression. We thank God for good health, but look how the person who was sick and now recovered, how s/he thanks Him differently.

4. Don't Get Stuck in Marah

"And they came to Elim, where were twelve wells of water, and threescore and ten palm trees: and they encamped there by the waters" (Exodus 15:27). Please note, before they got to Elim, they had to go through Marah. Don't get stuck in Marah, Elim awaits you. As we renew our minds, let us refuse to remain in a set place because we saw the hand of God demonstrated there. There is more to be known of God as we continue the journey together. You don't want to live wondering what you missed because you got stuck in Marah.

In Marah, the tree has no name but in Elim, we know the name and quantity of the trees (10 olive trees). Marah is where the pockets of blessings are seen. Many reside there because of their failure to realize that the Lord has provided an open window of heaven in Elim. Don't settle for the crumbs in Marah and not get to the table prepared for you in Elim.

Unfortunately many have been tricked into believing that staying in Marah is a sign of being grateful. But hear me, as we renew our minds: staying in Marah and enjoying the crumbs are actually a demonstration of ingratitude. It is a rejection of the blessings prepared in advance at Elim. Pursue your Elim. The challenges you endured in Marah, will not be seen in Elim.

Compare Marah to Elim. In Marah they complained about the lack of water. In Marah, they had bitter water turned to sweet water. In Elim, they had twelve wells of water and ten palm trees. A major take away is: *despite all the bitterness, challenges and the attacks of the enemy we face, if we remain faithful and obedient to God, he will bring us through to receive His blessings that He already has in store for us.*

MIND RENEWAL KEYS

In this chapter on "Marah to Elim" we have shared some Mind Renewal keys to help you to become a better person. Here is a summary of these keys that you can apply to your life daily or as the circumstances arise. Read and meditate on them. Pray and declare them over your life to walk in the victory God has prepared for you.

1. Be specific in your asking.
2. Not every provision equates to solution.
3. Hear this: lack, insufficiency and poverty can be idols because that mindset has been elevated above the Word and knowledge of who God is.
4. Replace the maybe attitude with that of assurance and certainty. I know God is my answer.
5. Stop trying to dictate to God how you want it done!
6. Your Destiny Helpers might not come with titles and prestige.
7. See yourself from the lenses of God.
8. Your pain is not insignificant. Use it as your propelling agent that connects you to your Destiny Helpers.
9. Despite the bitterness and challenges, your pre-prepared blessings await you.

Chapter 17:
Overcome

"Crisis is a powerful tool if used effectively and is able to pull at the creativity of each human."

—Leostone Morrison

After a rehearsal with God, it was time for Moses to see the hand of God being with him. God prepared him before he went. Let's imagine if he was not trained or processed, how he would have run away from Pharaoh when his rod turned into a snake.

And Moses and Aaron went in unto Pharaoh, and they did so as the LORD had commanded: and Aaron cast down his rod before Pharaoh, and before his servants, and it became a serpent. Then Pharaoh also called the wise men and the sorcerers: now the magicians of Egypt, they also did in like manner with their enchantments. For they cast down every man his rod, and they became serpents: but Aaron's rod swallowed up their rods (Exodus 7:10-12).

That is the Supreme Power of God. This shows Divine control over every situation. Great is the mystery of God. This account was one of the first that highlighted to me that Satan has powers. Moses's rod became a snake. Pharaoh's magicians also threw down their rods and they became snakes. As we renew our minds, let us first be cognizant of this truth: *the power of God supersedes the power of Satan.*

Secondly, do not be sign chasers as there are counterfeit miracles. Let's slow down. This is serious business. Pharaoh's magicians did the same thing that Aaron did. This has plagued the church and the world. Evil workers are parading as men and women with the anointing of the Holy Spirit. People are so desperate for a sign that the devil does not have to waste time making it look authentic. Sign seeking is not a new phenomenon. In Matthew 12:38-39, we see men asking Jesus for a sign.

Then certain of the scribes and of the Pharisees answered, saying, 'Master, we would see a sign from thee.' But he answered and said unto them, 'An evil and adulterous generation seeketh after a sign; and there shall no sign be given to it, but the sign of the prophet Jonas... (Matthew 12:38-39)

Aaron's snake overpowered the snakes of the magicians. They were no match although Aaron's snake was outnumbered. It was not in its regular place. Renew your mind in this wise, your victory is not dependent upon a place of familiarity but upon the strength of your commander. The Lord wants to reassure you. "Don't be perplexed by the numbers against you or the odds against you." The greater the odds, the greater the magnificence of your victory. As it is, you are the least likely victor but rest in the knowledge that "... greater is he that is in you, than he that is in the world" (1 John 4:4b).

Look at the story of David and Goliath. Here the words of Goliath in 1 Samuel 17:43-44.

And the Philistine said unto David, Am I a dog that thou comest to me with staves? And the Philistine cursed David by his gods. And the Philistine said to David, Come to me, and I will give thy flesh unto the fowls of the air, and to the beasts of the field.

Here the words of King Saul in 1 Samuel 17:33.

And Saul said to David, Thou art not able to go against this Philistine to fight with him: for thou art but a youth, and he a man of war from his youth.

Here the words of Eliab, David's brother, in 1 Samuel 17:28.

And Eliab his eldest brother heard when he spake unto the men; and Eliab's anger was kindled against David, and he said, Why camest thou down hither? and with whom hast thou left those few sheep in the wilderness? I know thy pride, and the naughtiness of thine heart; for thou art come down that thou mightest see the battle. The enemy (Goliath), King (Saul) and

Eliab (David's brother) all saw him as insignificant. Eliab belittled him bitterly, when he classified David's job as looking over (few) sheep.

Let yesterday be the last day you accept the perception that you are insignificant from the enemy, leadership or family members.

You might not have a high profile job or position in the church, in your family or society, but that's not where your worth, value or significance comes from. Please note, the size of your enemy is a testimony of your mandate, purpose, anointing. For David, it was Goliath who defied an entire army. For Moses, it was Pharaoh who was seen as a god and had almost two million Jews in captivity.

Do not quit because of the size of your enemy, your problems, situation etc. Know that you are equipped to handle it. God has pre-approved your victory. *You are not fighting to be victorious; you entered already the victor.* Go in the strength of the Lord.

KNOW YOUR POWER

Moses was tending to his father-in-law's flock when he had an encounter. He saw some bush on fire but they were not burnt. This captivated his mind and he drew closer to see what was happening. From the bush, a voice—the voice of God spoke to him. God told him he was sending him to deliver His children out of bondage in Egypt. In getting Moses to understand that he was not going in his own strength, God gave him a rehearsal of what will happen in Egypt.

And the LORD said unto him, what is that in thine hand? And he said, A rod. And he said, Cast it on the ground. And he cast it on the ground, and it became a serpent; and Moses fled from before it. And the Lord said unto Moses, Put forth thine hand, and take it by the tail. And he put forth his hand, and caught it, and it became a rod in his hand (Exodus 4:2-4).

In the rehearsal God showed Moses that He God was able to give life to that which had no life and he had the power to take back life. He taught Moses that for him to be successful, maintaining relationship and obedience are a must. Moses had to conquer his fear and obey. Obedience must supersede fear. In the rehearsals Moses saw his hand whole, then lepros, then whole again. This, I believe God used to symbolize Israel. They were whole then got sick (slavery) and now they are about to be made whole again.

After the rehearsal came the meeting we see in Exodus 7:10-12 with Moses and Aaron before Pharaoh. This was not the rehearsal. What God did not tell Moses was that after your rod turns into a snake, Pharaoh's magicians will do the same. That was not a part of the rehearsal. Hear this, God never promised to tell or give you everything all at once. God's teaching and giving do not stop at rehearsal. The rehearsal is just enough to increase your faith to get you on board. What do you do when that which was not in the preliminaries pops up? In track and field, they call it the heats. You must continue to trust God. He brought you this far, He will complete the journey.

When the reality supersedes the rehearsal, keep calm. As I meditated, this point was strong. Keep calm. Don't allow the enemy's noise and show of strength to rob you of the stability of the promise. Keep calm, God's got this. To you, it is a surprise that they are able to turn their rods into snakes, but to God, it's not. God is fully aware of their limited power. When you see the enemy demonstrating power, keep calm. Don't be perturbed, disturbed, become doubtful and fearful instead, keep calm. Speak to yourself right now: "Keep calm. Remain calm!"

Moses' rod swallowed the rods of the magicians. This was victory number one. You need to look back at some past victories. The same God who secured those victories is the same God with you today. Rejoice! You were the only one who was surprised. God knew what the magicians could do, they knew what they could do, and you did not know what they could do. It doesn't stop there. God knows what He can do and what He will use you to do it. So *Keep Calm.*

God's power was demonstrated as the superior power. As you continue this journey of life, ensure that you are on the winning side.

And Aaron stretched out his hand over the waters of Egypt, and the frogs came up, and covered the land of Egypt. And the magicians did so with their enchantments, and brought up frogs upon the land of Egypt (Exodus 8:6–7).

Aaron obeyed God and His power was demonstrated by the frogs coming up on the land from the waters.

Look carefully. The magicians did their arts and brought up frogs too. In other words, they were saying, "that's nothing; we can match whatever you do." What does this tell us? Let us not be deceived, the enemy has the power to do signs and wonders. That's how he is able to deceive many. One such manner is the counterfeiting of the work of God.

Remember, when Moses threw down his rod and it became a snake, the magicians did the same also. This is power from two different sources. However, Moses' snake destroyed the magician's snakes. This demonstrates the superior power of God. To which source are you connected? We as children of God must understand that our arch enemy and his kingdom are inferior to the kingdom where we are citizens. Therefore, we not only have superior power but the authority to use that power over the kingdom of darkness. This is the position from which you do warfare.

It's not a place of questioning if we're going to win, but knowing that the enemy is no match for us. Renew your mind with this, when the enemy attacks you, he is actually out of his league. My God! Please understand this, you're not fighting to be victorious, that's already decided. Don't be baffled or bemused by the works of the kingdom of darkness. Know for certainty, they are no match. Watch this:

Then Pharaoh called for Moses and Aaron, and said, 'Intreat the LORD, that he may take away the frogs from me, and from my people; and I will let the people go, that they may do sacrifice unto the LORD' (Exodus 8:8).

To show strength and superiority, the magicians did not need to bring up more frogs, what they needed to do was to get rid of the frogs. But they couldn't. Pharaoh acknowledged God's superior power and asked Moses to beg God to remove the frogs. The enemy shall know that you operate at a higher standard. Here is a Mind Renewal truth you need to employ, *the enemy cannot undo what God has done in your life*. My God! Praise God! You are designed to win, you have the victory. The enemy had to beg for a break, but that we will not do. There will be no break; we are always attacking knowing that the battle is already won.

If you are fearful of the enemy undoing what God has done, stop that. Trust God. Philippians 1:6 says God will complete what He has started. God did not start your healing process to leave you midway. If God blessed you with the job, Satan cannot take it from you. Begin to dictate through the use of your divine authority how this is going to work out. Get aggressive. The passive Christianity is not going to work... Not in this age. The devil is a liar.

David said it nicely in response to Goliath's ranting, and having the army of Israel running from him in 1 Samuel 17:45-47.

Then said David to the Philistine, Thou comest to me with a sword, and with a spear, and with a shield: but I come to thee in the name of the LORD of hosts, the God of the armies of Israel, whom thou hast defied. This day will the LORD deliver thee into mine hand, and I will smite thee, and take thine head from thee; and I will give the carcasses of the host of the Philistines this day unto the fowls of the air, and to the wild beasts of the earth; that all the earth may know that there is a God in Israel. And all this assembly shall know that the LORD saveth not with sword and spear: for the battle is the LORD's, and he will give you into our hands (1 Samuel 17:45-47).

Let's slow down. Battles are lost easily. It takes more to win than to lose. The battle was never between Pharaoh and Moses or David and Goliath. They were between Jehovah God and the gods of Egypt and the Philistines. The reason why we have not been seeing more victories is because we have been fighting a spiritual battle in the fleshly realm.

Look at Exodus 7:1, And the LORD said unto Moses, "See, I have made thee a god to Pharaoh: and Aaron thy brother shall be thy prophet." Here God elevated Moses before he went in. Pay attention closely. This promotion was not in the physical realm; it was in the spiritual realm. There are many types of elevation, but none surpasses that of the spiritual realm. Moses did not see an increase in salary, in friendship, no party etc., and his promotion came from above. When God gives us a word, we must follow it closely. God did not say I have made you into a god. Moses was god only to Pharaoh.

Let me hasten to caution us to stay within the parameters of our promotion. If you are elevated to deliver a word, deliver as you received. Do not add or subtract. Be careful. We saw earlier, that Moses was the only one who did not know the magicians were able to turn their rods into snakes. God knew, the magicians knew. Now, God and Moses both are knowledgeable that God has elevated Moses to be a god over Pharaoh. Guess what, neither Pharaoh nor his magicians knew.

Let's renew our minds understanding that God will not give you an assignment for which He has not equipped you. You should not wait until you know the complete plan of God before you obey. Instead, you obey each instruction as they are given. Whatever God has mandated you to do, you can rest assured, you are not enlisted to fail.

USE WHAT YOU HAVE

A regrettable amount of time is wasted as persons wait for their big break... waiting for the tide to change. Believing the grass is greener on the other side, we compare ourselves and dream of living like how we see others flaunting. Always echoing the sentiment, "if." If I was born rich, bright, lived in another country and the list goes on. What we fail to recognize is , that which we have is sufficient to be used. As we renew our minds, let us arrive at the place where we are convicted in using what we have.

Now there cried a certain woman of the wives of the sons of the prophets unto Elisha, saying, Thy servant my husband is dead; and thou knowest that thy servant did fear the Lord: and the creditor is come to take unto him my two sons to be bondmen.
And Elisha said unto her, What shall I do for thee? tell me, what hast thou in the house? And she said,

Thine handmaid hath not any thing in the house, save a pot of oil (2 Kings 4:1-2).

Jehovah asked Moses a similar question when he expressed unbelief. God said, "What is it you have in your hand?" (Exodus 4:2). Elijah said to the widow woman, "what do you have in your house?" Renew your mind with this truth, whatever you have use it! Use what God has given to you. Can you sing? Sing. Can you dance? Dance. Are you an entrepreneur? Do business.

Today in the name of Jesus Christ of Nazareth, I declare the self-defeating nuisance of believing you don't have what it takes to accomplish your purpose be totally destroyed right now. For too long, we have been living in a prison of comparison and competition. The spirit of comparison has lied to us, and we have believed its lie for too long. You don't need to have everything Mary has to succeed. Is it possible for us to change our thinking to: "With all that I'm equipped with, Mary requires far more to accomplish the same." In other words, you don't need all of what others have to accomplish the same or more than what they have acquired. Use what you have.

As you compare yourself to others, what you have might seem insufficient. You never completed high school, you don't have a degree, you have failed at marriage, and you are terrible at finances. *Stop focusing on what you don't have, rather, on what you have.* Get this, you are equipped with more than you know. Refuse to let lack or crisis force you to a parking place. God has given you a creative mind. Use it.

Crisis is a powerful tool if used effectively and is able to pull at the creativity of each human. What is your crisis pulling out of you? It's inside... it just needs to be extracted. See yourself as a driver who has somewhere you must go, a task to be completed and a purpose to be fulfilled. Of course, you will have obstacles, but press along, press along.

Society says you need all of what the others have, but all you truly need is a surrendered mind to Jesus. Refuse to be neutralized by the insufficiencies of the natural realm, you function between two realms. The spirit realm is your first. What does the spirit realm say about you? There is a high calling on persons to reach families, communities and nations. What God has given to you cannot be contained by you alone. Nations are waiting. I see enlarged territories and borders. The discomfort and un-settledness might just be an indication that your space of influence is too small. My God! Persons are waiting for you. Yes, you. Use what you have.

A dear friend of mine cried out to God asking him about her financial situation. She said, "Lord I have been faithful to you, I pay my tithes, keep myself holy, I've rejected evil, so why is it I'm having it so hard?" and the Lord responded, "what happened to the songs?" Truth is the Lord has blessed her with a beautiful singing voice, the anointing to deliver and He gave her dozens of songs.

Essentially, what God said to her is this: "I have already given to you that which you need to elevate yourself out of financial crises." The present state you are in is all your doing. It reminds me of God saying to Joshua as he cried out to him after Israel lost the battle against Ai.

God said "get up off thy face, it is not time to cry, it's time to act" (Joshua 7:6-10).

Let us renew our minds to this place, wherever our gifts and talents lay, let us purpose to do our best. Be the best carpenter, teacher, lawyer, street cleaner, and window wiper. This story reported in the Jamaica Star newspaper on October 20, 2018, illustrates this point.

At age 11, Dwayne Whittaker ran away from home and was begging on the street.

He felt uncomfortable doing this and set out to find ways to make money. The sight of men wiping windshields for a living caught his eyes and he decided to start doing something that made him feel a sense of accomplishment. He was not attending school and so for years Whittaker wiped windshields and saved his money for a big day. Years later, he enrolled himself in the HEART Institute and did a data entry course. From then, his life seemed to make a turn for the better. Not forgetting the way he started, Whittaker said, that he never abandoned windshield wiping because it is putting food on the table and even sending himself and his son to school.

Now enrolled at the University of the West Indies and doing a three-month course in film production, Whittaker said that he is happy about his enrolment and is working to get his certification in that field.

Whitaker is one whom we would say got a bad hand, but he used that bad hand and is presently at the University of the West Indies studying. Many persons who have well-paying jobs have the desire to study but have not. He showed us that your place of origin does not have to determine your journey or your closing. Whitaker showed us how to use what we have.

STOP PRETENDING

As we pursue a renewed mind, we need to remove ourselves from the pain of pretending. With God you don't have to pretend, just be who you are, which is far easier than pretending. We can be open with the Holy Spirit. Share our dreams, concerns and shortcomings. Our stress points are areas of failures. We don't have to pretend to have it all together. Wait, don't you believe the Holy Spirit knows that you don't have it all together? I don't have it all together. I wish I did and while I'm not where I would love to be, I'm glad I'm not where I used to be.

There is a mighty deliverance that comes with being openly honest with where you are on your journey... when you don't have to pretend to wear a size 6 when you're at a size 9 shoe. There is joy in knowing that you're still a masterpiece being developed. You are still a work in progress.

I still have some rough edges. But guess what, I'm on the potter's wheel. The rough edges serve as a reminder that, God is still moulding and shaping me. You have your rough edges too and maybe some cracks. But guess what? You don't have to pretend anymore. Continue working on it. As you avail yourself to God, He will help you. Thomas said until I see the scars, I won't believe. That is where he was. He did not believe and expressed his doubt.

Jesus addressed Thomas's position. Thomas's doubt was removed. Many of us have doubts and fears but we pretend and so they live with us for years. Doubt and fear become our neighbours. Did you know pretending is a lie? Yes, it is. We live with the intent to cause persons to believe our pretence. That's deception. We have been pretending for so long, we've forgotten who we truly are... too many different faces.

Where am I? Where are you? Now, here is a rough one. Who are persons in love with? Which version of you? Who stood at the altar and said "I do?" Why can't your children and spouse enjoy the version of you that your pastor and church family adore? A lot of marriages fail because as we get comfortable, we begin to remove the mask that stood at the altar and said "I do." Now, the partner is wondering, "who is this person?" Confusion sets in, and we say the person changed. This is not really a change, just the truth being revealed.

Wait Brother Leo, if I take off my masks then persons will know I don't know how to receive compliments or love. I don't trust, I'm broken, etc. It's easier to pretend. I'm not sure you will like the unmasked me, but that's who I am. Will you still love me when you see my cracks, my flaws, weaknesses, etc.? Will you still love me when you realize I'm not always flowing in the anointing? Truth is, you never took the time to know me. You loved the anointing. So let us cut the pretending. This is me. I have some flaws that I'm working on. I'm not perfect. I am not perfect but I just want to be more like Jesus. So going forward, I'm taking off the mask. I'm what you see. If you see a flaw, if you can help, please help. If you're looking a next hot gossip, move along. If we follow these Mind Renewal keys, we will overcome!

MIND RENEWAL KEYS

In this chapter on "Overcome" we have shared some Mind Renewal keys to help you to become a better person. Here is a summary of these keys that you can apply to your life daily or as the circumstances arise. Read and meditate on them. Pray and declare them over your life to walk in the victory God has prepared for you.

1. The power of God supersedes the power of Satan.
2. People are so desperate for a sign that the devil does not have to waste time making it look authentic.
3. Your victory is not dependent upon a place of familiarity but upon the strength of your commander.
4. The greater the odds, the greater the magnificence of your victory.
5. The size of your enemy is a testimony of your mandate, purpose and anointing.

6. God knows what He can do and what He will use you to do. So Keep Calm.
7. When the enemy attacks you, he is actually out of his league.
8. The enemy cannot undo what God has done in your life.
9. The reason why we have not been seeing more victories is because we have been fighting a spiritual battle in the fleshly realm.
10. Escape the prison of comparison and competition.
11. Stop focusing on what you don't have, rather fous on what you have. Use what you have.
12. Get this, you are equipped with more than you know.
13. Refuse to let lack or crisis force you to a parking place.
14. Refuse to be neutralized by the insufficiencies of the natural realm. You function between two realms.
15. The discomfort and un-settledness might just be an indication that your space of influence is too small.
16. We need to remove ourselves from the pain of pretending.
17. Experiences are capable of opening your awareness and senses to the previously unknown.
18. Cockroaches leave where there is no food provided.

Chapter 18:

Coming to Yourself

"Become not what you decided to settle for, but what you were meant to be." —Leostone Morrison

Like the prodigal son, of Luke chapter 15, I lost everything that I trusted in and loved. Poor decisions and impatience had gushed me into waters for which I was unprepared. Then emptiness forced me to realize that I did not belong in that position. I tried to make it without God and was rudely awakened to the fact that I cannot. You, too, have made your blunders and like the prodigal son you need to kill pride and the desire to cast blame in order to rise again. You must purpose in your heart to arise and go back to the Father. It is time for you to come to yourself and embrace home—the place where all the supplies for your needs await you.

And he would fain have filled his belly with the husks that the swine did eat: and no man gave unto him. And when he came to himself, he said, How many hired servants of my father's have bread enough and to spare, and I perish with hunger! I will arise and go to my father, and will say unto him, Father, I have sinned against heaven, and before thee (Luke 15:16-18).

As you come to yourself and your mind is renewed, please note, experience is a master teacher. Experiences are capable of opening your awareness and senses to the previously unknown. However, lessons taught can easily be missed. From vs 16b, "no man gave to him" a powerful lesson can be learned. You may have been there too. You gave to them, you were there for them but now you are in a bind, they have all gone. No one comes to your aid. Be conscious of this truth, they never saw you, they saw your gifts and what you had to offer. They were never into you, only what they could get from you. Now you have nothing, why should they stay?

The mistake you made was not ensuring the friend-ship was reciprocated. It was one-sided all this time. But you were too in love to see. Tell that friend "no" sometimes, don't dial their number (see if they call) watch the body language as you share a victory. Take stock of the takers versus the givers. Renew your mind in this wise, is this friendship a need or a supply?

Let's look at the text again in Luke 15:17: "And when he came to himself, he said, How many hired servants of my fathers have bread enough and to spare, and I per-ish with hunger!" The writing here suggests that there was a separation between the young man and himself.

In other words, he was functioning outside of his normal self. It means therefore that his behaviour and actions were being influenced by an unseen force. We need to understand that some behaviour that we see being demonstrated are not normal, but are coming from negative influences.

Let's bring it home. Think of your actions. Are you acting like yourself or are you being influenced by negative forces? Is your spirit, mind and body in cohesion or in sync? Are we functioning as one person or as a disjointed being? As a man thinks, so is he. Much attention needs to be placed on what or who is influencing our thoughts. When the Holy Spirit tells you to do something and your body stands in disagreement, that's a classic example of a disjointed being. What is needed is total surrender of our thoughts to the Holy Spirit.

The truth is many of us need to come to ourselves. The son was out of himself from he began thinking about asking his father for his inheritance. He stayed in that place until he wasted all of it and was now broke and eating among the pigs. This is a dangerous place to remain. The war will be to prevent you from coming to yourself. The enemy will try to keep you disjointed. A disjointed person will never succeed. A disjointed person will have trouble discerning the voice of the Holy Spirit vs. the voice of demons. Hear what the Holy Spirit is saying, for example, when a man and a woman get married, they become one. Unfortunately, there are marriages that are still disjointed. They are not themselves.

Did you know, if you speak badly about your spouse, you're speaking badly about yourself? If you curse your spouse, you're cursing yourself. After this, you ask for prayer but what you need is repentance. There are marriages failing because the partners have been working against the marriage. We have to change that. Come back to oneness. You have been fasting for the person to change but fast for your change. The young man came back to himself. He got his deliverance. His eyes were opened. The cloud of disjointedness was removed.

Father in the name of Jesus, I pray, bind and remove every dark cloud that has been strategically positioned to cause blindness and self-destruction. Watch the strategy of the enemy. Please don't miss it. The enemy set him up against himself. He became his biggest enemy. My God! He was ambushed. Listen, if the enemy can get you to fight against yourself, his work is done.

In Mark 3:25, Jesus said a house divided among itself cannot stand. Identify the division and crush it. Refuse to let self-division continue to reign. Come back to the unity of self. Order is needed in our being to function properly and effectively. "And be not conformed to this world: but be ye transformed by the renewing of your mind, that ye may prove what is that good, and acceptable, and perfect, will of God" (Romans 12:2). We will come back to ourselves as our minds are renewed and transformed. Speak change to your mind. "Mind, I speak to you right now. For too long you've been acting funny, but I call you into submission and transformation to and by the word of God today, in Jesus' name."

Hear this, it's not enough to get your deliverance, you need to maintain it. He got his deliverance when he came to himself. He decided to maintain it when he chose to go back home, back to the source. If you've been getting deliverance from the same thing over and over, you need to maintain your deliverance. It's the deliverance of your mind. It's time to stop seeing yourself as insufficient, thinking you don't measure up, that you belong in the back. Stop settling for less. You deserve the best. Accept that God has qualified you. Tell that thought goodbye. If the enemy succeeds in locking your mind, he will never have to fight you again. You are more than what the enemy wants you to believe.

The enemy wants you to live below the standard God has prepared for you. He came to himself. What pushed him to come to himself? It was his brokenness and the favor of God. By becoming broke, experiencing the famine, working with the swines, friends forsaking him, no one gave anything unto him... It was rough but it was the favour of God. In coming to himself he acknowledged that he was at a bad place. There was no room to pretend to have it all in sync. As you renew your mind, refuse to pretend yourself away from your breakthrough.

One night my son asked me, "what do I have to tell him?" I said, "invest in your tomorrow." What you are living today is what was sowed in the past. The decisions you make today determine the future you live. Therefore, come back to yourself today and cease masquerading in the filth of your folly. Invest in your mind. Renew your mind.

HURTING ENOUGH TO CHANGE

In one of his motivational talks, Les Brown shared a story. A boy and his father went for a walk. They were new to the community. They saw an elderly man sitting on the verandah with his dog lying on the ground beside him. As they got closer, the boy realized that the dog was groaning. Concerned, they asked the elderly man, "what was wrong?" The man replied, "he is lying on a nail that is hurting him. However, the pain is not sufficient to get him to move."

The dog desired a position that came with a price, pain. His deliverance was up to him. It depended on his willingness to move. He was lying down but not resting... lying down in pain. Like this dog, some of us are lying down on some big nails. We have been in the situation for so long that we have gotten acclimatized. Rather than getting to a place of rest, we lay groaning in pain. As I discussed this truth with a friend, she said, "what if the pain is all the person knows?" This is their normal. To the outsider, it seems as abuse but this is how the person was cultured. Your pain might just be someone's normal. In this case, Mind Renewal is needed.

Hear the Word of the Lord, "God has prepared a place of rest for you. You can have the nail removed or you be removed from the place where the pain is. You're not confined to the pain." The dog had a relationship with the man, and so wanted to be close to him. However, being near meant undergoing abuse. If you are hanging onto an abusive relationship it's hurting you perpetually, but I guess like the dog, it's not hurting enough. In renewing our mind, how should we pray? Should we pray for the pain to be increased until it becomes unbearable or pray that the person comes to a place where the decision is made to escape the pain?

The prodigal son came back to himself as the pain became unbearable. You have to take back your rights. Refuse to let the abuse from others determine how you act, think and respond. Not taking charge of your fate is one of the enemy's ways of allowing you to question your identity. Do you remember who you are? You are a child of God (John 1:12). Start speaking it to yourself until you believe it and then act it out—child of God. You must decide to take no more. No more lying on the nails!

EXPRESS YOUR RENEWED MIND

A renewed mind will be afforded opportunities to express wealth. In the account of the prodigal son, we see a rich father who was hurt by the request of his youngest son but was willing to put aside his hurt and pain, when his son returned home. How do we treat those who have treated us badly, wasted our hard labour and now return in distress? We sometimes feel used. If they were not in a crisis, then we would not have heard from them. You might just be correct.

However, when we understand that God allowed the battering to drive them back to safety, when they return we should at least partner with God and help them to find rest. There is a place where restoration is the required medicine, not further beatings. I came to you because I'm battered. I don't need another battering.

This is where we have to put aside our hurts and pain and administer healing. Truth is, after being healed, the person might not stick around. And that's ok. Don't try to force someone to stay where they don't want to. Express your renewed mind as you heal, restore and release. I love how Naomi in the book of Ruth did it. She helped her daughters-in-law through their time of grief and then told them, it's time for us to separate, go back to your family. One of her daughters-in-law left (Orpah) and the other (Ruth) stayed. Understand that the Orpahs will go and the Ruths will stay. Never try to get Orpah to play the role of Ruth. Orpah's time in your story is over. She is not ungrateful. She did what she was assigned to do. Heal, restore, now release.

The rich father restored his son above what the son was prepared for. He restored him to sonship although the son was prepared to be like a hired servant. He was restored to his former place. As you renew your mind, you are being restored to your rightful place. You are becoming not what you decided to settle for, but what you were meant to be.

MIND RENEWAL KEYS

In this chapter on "Coming to Yourself" we have shared some Mind Renewal keys to help you to become a better person. Here is a summary of these keys that you can apply to your life daily or as the circumstances arise. Read and meditate on them. Pray and declare them over your life to walk in the victory God has prepared for you.

1. Experience is a master teacher.
2. A disjointed person will never succeed.
3. Refuse to let self-division continue to reign.
4. If the enemy succeeds in locking your mind, he will never have to fight you again.
5. Cease masquerading in the filth of your folly.
6. Your pain might just be someone's normal.
7. A renewed mind will be afforded opportunities to express wealth.
8. When we understand that God allowed the battering to drive them back to safety, when they return we should at least partner with God and help them to find rest.
9. Put aside our hurts and pain and administer healing.
10. Heal, restore and release.
11. Never try to get Orpah to play the role of Ruth.
12. Pursue not what you decided to settle for, but what you were meant to be.
13. You will not conquer that which you have not confronted.

AFTERWORD:

GOING FORWARD

Let's change our minds to live intentionally. Do not be merely carried away by the wind but commence a journey of being purpose-driven. Chase a better you by the renewal of your mind. We have some bonus keys for you. Use them to become a better YOU.

1. **Remind yourself daily that you are a child of God.** Before the foundation of the world, God loved you. This should be enough to remember that before there was anything he loved YOU.

2. **Think positively about yourself.** Make a concerted effort, to remove the negatives and embrace the positive you. For years negativity has reigned and rained its onslaught of destiny breaking, self-defeating and purpose killing devices upon

you. But going forward, as you renew your mind, you're going to fight back and take charge. The positive you is more attractive, goal-oriented and purpose-driven. Understand and embrace that you are not worse than anyone, you are a beautiful/handsome, intelligent person. You are not what others say or think but one who has the power to make or break self with what you say or think.

3. **Confront your fears:** To adequately renew your mind, you must be willing to confront your fears. Jonathan and Melissa Helser's did a song, "I'm no longer a slave to fear." For years fear has dictated your speech, walk and even your thoughts. Fear has prevented many multi-million dollar projects from being converted from an idea to actuality. What fear has you bound? It's time to be free. Your fear of public speaking or expressing your mind has prevented you from seeing your borders expanded. Renew your mind in this wise: "For God hath not given us the spirit of fear; but of power, and of love, and of a sound mind." (2 Timothy 1:7). Therefore, fear will keep you in the dark no more, as the light desperately awaits your wealth. Place your confidence in God, then you will conquer anything. Rest assured you will not conquer that which you have not confronted.

4. **Don't compare yourself with others:** This helped me a lot. I heard T.D. Jakes say it and I

embraced it completely. "If God wanted another T.D. Jakes, He would have made another." God wanted you, so he created you. Don't compare yourself to others or try to be like someone else. Be you. Let the unique you be expressed and known. Live this truth, "I am who God says I am. I am me, (put your name) Not Leo, not Mary, Sue, or Jane." Abort the desire to compare, and instead love on you.

5. **Develop strong self-confidence.** You can do it. You can go back to school, get that degree, succeed at marriage, be that motivational speaker or simply lose that weight you've desired to for so long. You can do it. Stop belittling yourself.

6. **Be grateful for everything you have:** A major transformation is becoming grateful for everything you have, family, financial status, the roof over your head, clothes to wear, food to eat and shoes to wear. You may not have a lot of money, but you have more than enough. You have been waiting for the big break while ignoring the small blessings.

7. **Speak positive words over yourself and others.** Remain calm and avoid negative outbursts about anyone including self, when angry or upset.

8. **Believe you can achieve:** For too long, you have doubted yourself. Believe that you can achieve

whatever you focus your mind to achieve. If your mental state is, *I can't do it* then you won't.

9. **Set measurable goals.** Have a plan and work to achieve that plan. Give yourself set deadlines.

10. **Get physically active again.** Stop telling yourself it's not worth it. Get up, get out and work out.

CLOSING PRAYER

I declare in the name of Jesus Christ that my mind will not back slide to where it has departed. I will become who God says I am. As I continue to renew my mind I refuse to be stuck at the caterpillar stage but will pursue the butterfly within me. I rejoice in the wealth of my spirit as it feeds from the reservoir of God. I'm no longer bound to the limitations of the physical realm and will gladly demonstrate the freedom of the Spirit. I declare I will fulfil my destiny by the help of the Holy Spirit.

I call forth all my Destiny Helpers to come in alignment with the word and will of God. I am not a failure, victory is my name. I am delivered from the errors of my past and bask in the bounty of my present as I simultaneously create the wealth of my future. I am no longer a product of my circumstances but a masterpiece of God. My mind is transformed, my life is transformed, and I am a new person. I will think, speak, and live from my renewed mind.

The old me has gone, and I embrace the new me, the renewed me.

REFERENCES

A Conversation with Wayne Dyer. (n.d.). Retrieved December 07, 2018, from https://www.drwaynedyer.com/press/conversation-wayne-dyer/

A Conversation with Wayne Dyer. (n.d.). Retrieved December 07, 2018, from https://www.drwaynedyer.com/press/conversation-wayne-dyer/

Bigun. (2006, February 16). *Wife is Unsaved*. Retrieved December 5, 2018, from https://www.christianforums.com/threads/wife-is-unsaved.2580693/

Cupbearer Definition and Meaning. Bible Dictionary. (n.d.). Retrieved December 4, 2018, from https://www.biblestudytools.com/dictionary/cupbearer/

Diamond DART-450 / TA-20 Trainer. (2018, December 30). Retrieved December 30, 2018, from https://thaimilitaryandasianregion.wordpress.com/2018/12/30/diamond-dart-450-ta-20-trainer/

Hills, C. (2016, May 04). *Ancient Story, Modern Message:* The Cracked Pot. Retrieved December 7, 2018, from https://www.tcmworld.org/ancient-story-modern-message-the-cracked-pot/

"I Have a Dream," Address Delivered at the March on Washington for Jobs and Freedom. (2019, January 25). Retrieved December 7, 2018, from https://kinginstitute.stanford.edu/king-papers/docu ments/i-have-dream-address-delivered-march-washington-jobs-and-freedom

Marcus Garvey Quotes. (n.d.). Retrieved December 8, 2018, from https://www.brainyquote.com/quotes/marcus_garv ey_365148

Marcus Garvey Quotes. (n.d.). Retrieved December 8, 2018, from https://www.brainyquote.com/quotes/marcus_garv ey_365148

Matthews, K. (2017, November 18). Cops launch probe after reviewing suicide video. Retrieved December 5, 2018, from http://www.loopjamaica.com/content/cops-launch-probe-after-reviewing-suicide-video

Promise. (n.d.). Retrieved December 25, 2018, from https://www.merriam-webster.com/dictionary/pro mise

Rampton, J. (2014, December 09). 15 Ways to Become a

Better Person. Retrieved December 5, 2018, from
https://www.inc.com/john-rampton/15-ways-to-
become-a-better-person.html

Reality | Definition of reality in English by Oxford
Dictionaries. (n.d.). Retrieved December 15, 2018,
from https://en.oxforddictionaries.com/defini-
tion/reality

Team, M. (2018, November 25). 13 Y-O Boy Committed
Suicide in St Mary; Video Found on Cellphone.
Retrieved December 17, 2018, from
https://newsbugmedia.com/world/19-ja-local/1350-
13-y-o-boy-committed-suicide-in-st-mary-video-
found-on-cellphone

Team, P. (2019, January 30). Barack Obama quotes
about change, education, and equality. Retrieved
December 04, 2018, from
https://everydaypowerblog.com/barack-obama-
quotes/

The Three Parts of Man—Spirit, Soul, and Body. (2018,
July 20). Retrieved December 07, 2018, from https://
blog.biblesforamerica.org/the-three-parts-of-man-
spirit-soul-and-body/

There can be no greater gift than that of giving one's
time & energy to help others without expecting
anything in return. (n.d.). Retrieved December 14,
2018, from http://quotes.yourdictionary.com/-
author/nelson-mandela/611449

Thomas Jefferson Quotes. (n.d.). Retrieved December 07, 2018, from https://www.brainyquote.com/authors/thomas_jefferson

ABOUT THE AUTHOR

The Jamaican born, Leo-
stone Peron Morrison, has
served as an Assistant Pastor, Guidance Counselor at
the Ministry of Education
in Jamaica, and Probation
Officer in St. Kitts and
Nevis. He is the founder of
Next Level Let's Climb
Bible Study Ministry. Bathroom cleaning was his first
ministry assignment.

He is a graduate of the Jamaica Theological Seminary
where he attained a Bachelors in Theology with a
minor in Guidance and Counselling. He acquired a
Diploma in Biblical Principles from Victory Bible
School and a Certificate from the International Accelerated Missions School. He is married and has four
sons and one daughter. To contact the author email
him at restorativeauthor@gmail.com.

Made in the USA
Middletown, DE
10 May 2022

65564885R10135